Book Publishing

IN THE

U·S·S·R

REPORTS OF THE DELEGATIONS
OF U.S. BOOK PUBLISHERS
VISITING THE U.S.S.R.

October 21 - November 4, 1970
August 20 - September 17, 1962

Second edition, enlarged

Harvard University Press
Cambridge, Massachusetts

Library of Congress Cataloging in Publication Data
Main entry under title:

Book publishing in the U. S. S. R.

The report of the 1970 delegation supplements and
brings up to date the material from the report of the
1962 delegation which was first published in 1963
under the same title.
  1. Book industries and trade--Russia.
I. Delegation of U. S. Book Publishers Visiting the
U. S. S. R. (1962) Book publishing in the U. S. S. R.
1971. II. Delegation of the U. S. Book Publishers
Visiting the U. S. S. R. (1970) Book publishing in
the U. S. S. R. 1971.
Z366.B585 1971   338.4'7'07050947   76-37283

ISBN 0-674-07874-8

Additional copies of this report may be
ordered at $4.95 postpaid from:

Harvard University Press
79 Garden Street
Cambridge, Massachusetts 02138

CONTENTS

Chapter

Page

1970 Report   1962 Report

		1970	1962
	Preface	1	63
I	Introduction	3	65
II	Organization of Book Publishing	6	68
III	Operation of a Publishing House	10	74
IV	Book Distribution	12	80
V	Statistics on Book Production and Prices	14	91
VI	Foreign Trade	17	100
VII	Book Manufacturing in the U.S.S.R.	18	108
VIII	Belles-Lettres	19	118
IX	Scientific and Technical Books	21	123
X	Textbooks for Elementary and Secondary Schools	23	128
XI	Children's Books	24	141
XII	Textbooks for Higher Education	26	144
XIII	Encyclopedia and Dictionary Publishing	27	147
XIV	Translations	32	151
XV	Authors' Royalties	34	161
XVI	Copyright	35	168
XVII	Epilogue		176
	Index		177
Appendixes		39	

TABLES

1970 Report

		Page
1	Type of Publishing--Books and Pamphlets, 1969	7
2	Book and Pamphlet Publishing in the Byelorussian S.S.R., 1969	8
3	U.S.S.R. Combined Book and Pamphlet Production, 1961 and 1969	15
4	U.S.S.R. Production 1969: Books, Pamphlets, Original Editions and Reprint Editions	16

1962 Report

1	Publishing Houses in the U.S.S.R. Ministry of Culture, 1961 Production	73
2	Production of Books and Pamphlets in the U.S.S.R.	98
3	Production of Priced and Unpriced Books and Pamphlets in the U.S.S.R.	98
4	Comparison of Book Prices, U.S.S.R. and U.S.A.	99
5	Exports of Publications, Stamps and Motion Pictures	103
6	Imports of Publications, Stamps and Motion Pictures	103
7	Exports of Books and Other Publications	104
8	Imports of Books and Other Publications	104
9	Exports of the U.S.S.R. of Books and Other Publications	105
10	Imports of the U.S.S.R. of Books and Other Publications	106
11	Printing Equipment Imports of the U.S.S.R.	107
12	Books and Pamphlets--Russian and U.S.S.R. Minority Authors of Belles-Lettres by Dates Authors were Active	122
13	Production of Textbooks, Programs and Guidance Literature	140
14	Book and Pamphlet Translations in the U.S.S.R. by Language Groups	157
15	Book and Pamphlet Translations in the U.S.S.R. from Foreign Languages	157
16	Books and Pamphlets--by Language	158
17	Translation of Complete Books in 1962 Catalog of the Publishing House of Foreign Literature	158

18   Most Popular Foreign Authors (Belles-Lettres)
      in U.S.S.R. 159

19   The Soviet All-Time Best Seller List of American
      Authors 159

20   Publication in U.S.S.R. of American Works in Fields
      Other Than Belles-Lettres During Postwar Period . . . 160

21   New and Old Scales of Authors' Royalties
      (RSFSR) 166

22   Books and Pamphlets--by Republic Where Published 167

Book Publishing
IN THE
U·S·S·R

REPORT OF THE DELEGATION
OF U.S. BOOK PUBLISHERS
VISITING THE U.S.S.R.

October 21 - November 4, 1970

Robert L. Bernstein   *Edward J. McCabe, Jr.*
Mark S. Carroll   *W. Bradford Wiley*
Robert W. Frase

W. Bradford Wiley
President
John Wiley and Sons, Inc.
605 Third Avenue
New York, New York 10016
Chairman, Association of American Publishers

Robert L. Bernstein
President
Random House
201 East 50th Street
New York, New York 10022
Vice Chairman, Association of American Publishers

Edward J. McCabe, Jr.
Chairman of the Board
Grolier Incorporated
575 Lexington Avenue
New York, New York 10022
Treasurer, Association of American Publishers

Mark S. Carroll
Director
Harvard University Press
79 Garden Street
Cambridge, Massachusetts 02138
Secretary, Association of American Publishers

Robert W. Frase
Vice President and Economist
Association of American Publishers
1826 Jefferson Place, N. W.
Washington, D. C. 20036

This account of book publishing in the U.S.S.R. consists of two parts. The second is an unchanged reprint of "Book Publishing in the U.S.S.R.," a report of a U. S. publishing delegation in 1962, which was published by the American Book Publishers Council, Inc. and the American Textbook Publishers Institute, Inc. in 1963 (Library of Congress catalog card number 63-12756), which is now out of print. So much of the basic pattern of the U.S.S.R. book trade has remained unchanged that on reporting on the visit of the second U. S. publishers delegation in October-November 1970 it seemed most practical to supplement the 1963 report with a briefer account, using the same chapter numbers and headings, which would highlight the changes in the eight years between the two visits and bring the statistical and factual information up to date. Thus, the first part of this publication constitutes the supplementary material for 1970.

We had the advantage in preparing the section for 1970, which was not true with respect to the earlier report, of a review by our hosts of the factual statements made in a draft of the manuscript, for which we are grateful. The authors, however, must take responsibility for all statements of fact and expressions of opinion in the 1970 part as well as in the 1962 part.

The highlights of changes noted in 1970 as compared with 1962, which are elaborated in the chapters which follow, are:

1. Organization. There was a complete reorganization beginning in 1963 of the control of publishing at the top, both at the national level in the U.S.S.R. and at the level of the Republics, with Press Committees of the U.S.S.R. centralizing the supervision of book publishing, printing and distribution.

2. Consolidation. The number of publishing houses was somewhat reduced by consolidations.

3. Output and Prices. The annual output of titles of books and pamphlets has grown very little since 1961 - just over 1%. Production of copies of books and pamphlets combined has

increased about 18% in these eight years, but the number of copies per capita - 5.55 in 1961 and 5.48 in 1969 - has remained constant. For priced books and pamphlets alone, the number of copies per capita in 1969 was exactly the same as in 1961 - 52 copies. These developments reflect the continuing scarcity of paper allocated to book production. The average price per title of those books and pamphlets sold has increased by about 17%, from 36 kopecks per copy in 1961 to 43 kopecks in 1969.

4. Statistics. As a result of the adoption of the 1964 UNESCO statistical standards for publishing,* much more detailed and comparable data are now provided in the annual statistical publication - Pechat' S.S.S.R. The most valuable new material for purposes of international comparisons is the separation of data on book and pamphlet output and on original, as contrasted with reprint, editions.

5. Book Printing. Great progress has been made in the last eight years in introducing more modern equipment in book manufacturing plants and increasing the quality of books produced.

6. Bookstores. A number of new bookstores of modern design have come into operation in recent years, especially in Moscow, some of which give the customer a much better opportunity to see and examine the stock.

7. International Copyright. Officials concerned with publishing, authorship and international trade with whom we met in 1970 seemed much better informed on the subject of international copyright conventions than their counterparts had been in 1962, as well as being more interested in discussing the pros and cons of U.S.S.R. membership in such conventions.

*Recommendation Concerning the International Standardization of Statistics Relating to Book Production and Periodicals.

I. INTRODUCTION

A second delegation of American publishers visited the U.S.S.R. under the provisions of the Cultural Exchange Agreement between the U.S.A. and the U.S.S.R. The exchange of delegations was proposed to the State Department in April, an aide memoire was presented to the Embassy of the U.S.S.R. in May and an agreement reached with the U.S.S.R. in August.

One stated objective was to bring up to date by revision, correction, addition and deletion, "Book Publishing in the U.S.S.R." issued in early 1963 as a Report of the Delegation of U. S. Publishers' visit to the U.S.S.R. in August and September 1962. Another important objective was to resume discussion of international copyright, and a third, international organizations and programs such as the International Publishers Association and International Book Year. The aide memoire, therefore, consisted of fifteen specific items as well as one miscellaneous heading. The report which follows became possible because the Press Committee of the U.S.S.R. graciously accepted our requests, and skillfully designed an itinerary and agenda.

The delegation of five was made up of the four officers of the Board of Directors of the Association of American Publishers: W. Bradford Wiley, Chairman; Robert L. Bernstein, Vice Chairman; Mark S. Carroll, Secretary; Edward J. McCabe, Jr., Treasurer; and Robert W. Frase, Vice President in charge of the Association's Washington, D. C. office. Mr. Wiley, the chairman of the delegation, and Mr. Frase, the secretary, were also members of the 1962 delegation.

Part of the preparation for the mission was a careful review of "Book Publishing in the U.S.S.R.," three reports by delegations of British publishers who visited the U.S.S.R. in 1964, 1966 and 1970, one prepared by the staff which accompanied the British Scientific Book Exhibit in Moscow in 1968, and "Scholarly Publishing in the U.S.S.R." by Marsh Jeanneret, Director, University of Toronto Press. The delegation met in London for two days to complete its working assignments. It also had the advantage of a luncheon meeting generously arranged by the British Publishers Association and attended by John Boon, Colin Eccleshare, Ronald Barker, Peter du Sautoy, Ian Parsons, and Robert Code-Holland, all members of one or another of the delegations to the U.S.S.R. Yurii B. Leonov, Vice President of Mezh-Kniga, during the Frankfurt Book Fair, provided an accurate weather forecast and especially sound advice on proper clothing.

From the time we arrived in Moscow the evening of October 21 until we departed the evening of November 4, we were the guests of the Press Committee, Council of Ministers of the U.S.S.R. We were provided with extremely comfortable hotel accommodations; ample and delicious food and beverages; transportation by car in and near the cities, and by train and plane between cities. The evening of our arrival we were warmly welcomed by members of the staff of the Press Committee including Deputy Chairman Grant Martynovich Martirosyan; Chief of the Foreign Relations Department Vladimir Ivanovich Naydenov; his assistant, Yurii Levin; and our translators, Vyacheslav Aleksandrovich Semyenov and Vladimir Luninsky. From the U. S. Embassy we were greeted by Roger Lydon, Press Officer and Mark Ramee, Book Officer who accompanied us by day in Moscow, and throughout the entire time away from Moscow.

Our work began and ended with meetings of two hours convened by Chairman Boris I. Stukalin in his office-conference room at the head-quarters of the State Committee. During the first meeting we were offered two itineraries and chose the one which took us to Minsk, capital of Byelorussia, for two days (Robert Frase directed an UNRRA Mission there in the fall of 1946) as well as Leningrad for three days. The itinerary was demanding because the U.S.S.R. is now on a five-day work week and there were only nine days for our work; nevertheless, we managed to keep twenty-five appointments, and also visited seven book-stores and one library. That first meeting ended with a thorough review of our specific and general objectives during which it was agreed that international copyright, international publishers organizations and International Book Year would be discussed more fully at our last meeting at the Press Committee in November.

At the final meeting on November 3 the delegation expressed its appreciation for being able to discuss copyright with interested and informed people at Mezh-Kniga, Novosti, the Writers' Union, and at publishers such as Mir, Nauka, Progress and the Encyclopedia Publishing

4

House. There was ample time to explain the general objectives of the
International Publishers Association, and its affiliated bodies, the
Scientific Technical and Medical Publishers Group and the Educational
Group. The discussion of International Book Year, initiated at UNESCO
by the U.S.S.R., led to an agreement to exchange information on plans
as they develop in each country.

The last major item on the agenda was a discussion of the visit
of the U.S.S.R. delegation to the U.S.A. in 1971. Much emphasis was
given to the wish that it would be led by Chairman Stukalin and that a
visit in May could include attending the first membership meeting of the
newly established Association of American Publishers.

The delegation not only enjoyed its working meetings, but also
had the pleasure of tours of Minsk and Leningrad, and associated
memorials, a visit to Zagorsk, two operas, two ballets, the circus, an
evening of documentary films and an afternoon in selected galleries in
the Hermitage. Chairman Stukalin welcomed us with a dinner, Deputy
Chairman Y. Y. Khomutov was host at a farewell luncheon, and Chargé
d'Affaires Mrs. Boris Klosson honored the delegation with a reception.

From arrival until departure we had the advantage of skilled
translators, Messrs. Semyenov and Leninsky, whose linguistic competence
reflected their regular careers in publishing. In return for their
invaluable contribution to the delegation's efforts, we introduced them
to American colloquialisms. Mr. Naydenov accompanied and assisted us
on the trip to Minsk and Leningrad. Mr. Mark Ramee, a Second Secretary
at the Embassy, was exceedingly helpful throughout our visit. Mr.
Herbert S. Okun, Deputy Director of the Office of Soviet Union Affairs,
Department of State, who accompanied the 1962 delegation, provided
advice and guidance both in advance of departure and during an informal
meeting in Spaso House. Our sincere thanks go to them.

This report, like the earlier one, is the work of all members
of the delegation.

II.   THE ORGANIZATION OF BOOK PUBLISHING

Since 1964 the control of book publishing has been centralized in the Press Committee of the Council of Ministers of the U.S.S.R. There are parallel committees for films and for broadcasting.   In addition the Press Committee is responsible for book distribution and book printing.

When these organizational changes were made in 1964 there was also a certain amount of consolidation of publishing houses. Thus, the top structure of the book trade in the U.S.S.R. described in our 1962 report has become much more centrally organized and controlled.

The present organization and personnel of the Press Committee is as follows:

Officials

Chairman	Boris Ivanovich STUKALIN
Deputy Chairmen	Ye. Ye. KHOMUTOV
	Grant Martynovich MARTIROSYAN
Members	Boris Antonovich KORCHAGIN
	Ivan Petrovich KOROVKIN
	Anatoliy Nikitich KOSTAKOV
	V. G. MOCHALOV
	A. P. RYBIN
	I. I. CHKHIKVISHVILI

Administrators

Chief, Main Administration for Capital Construction	Yevgeniy Pavlovich POSTNIKOV
Chief, Main Administration for Material-Technical Supply and Marketing	Boris Antonovich KORCHAGIN
Chief, Main Administration of Republic and Oblast' Publishing Houses	V. G. MOCHALOV
Chief, Finance Department	Ivan Petrovich KOROVKIN
Chief, Foreign Relations Department	V. I. NAYDENOV
Chief, Legal Department	Vasiliy KAMYSHEV
Chief Editor for Scientific and Technical Literature	Vasiliy Vasil'yevich YEZHKOV
Chief Editor for Sociopolitical Literature	Arseniy Sergeyevich MAKHOV
Chief, Production Administration	Grigoriy Khaimovich SHAPOSHNIKOV
Chief, Propaganda Section	A. BORODINA

At the Republic level (Ukrainian SSR, Uzbec SSR, etc.) there are also Press Committees attached to the Council of Ministers of the Republics. The functions of these Press Committees parallel those of the national Press Committee.

Central Publishing Houses

The national or All Union publishing houses of the U.S.S.R. fall into three categories with respect to their relationship to the Press Committee:

1. Those subject only to the Press Committee
2. Those subject both to the Press Committee and other organizations such as ministries
3. Those subject only to other organizations.

As shown in the table below, publishing houses subject to the Press Committee account for a high proportion not only of national publishing but total publishing in the U.S.S.R.

Table 1
Type of Publishing
Books and Pamphlets
1969

	Number of books and pamphlet titles	Printings in thousands of copies
T o t a l	74,587	1,315,721
1. Publishing houses of the Press Committee, Council of Ministers of the U.S.S.R., including		
Central	7,463	247,847
Republican	13,132	635,043
Other	5,822	76,296
2. Publishing houses of dual subordination, including		
Central	623	3,152
Republican	1,772	14,831
Other	792	18,449
3. Publishing houses of public organizations and departments		208,416
Central	9,260	57,385
Republican	241	1,161
4. Other organizations, establishments	35,482	110,526

Source: Table 43, Pechat' S.S.S.R. for the year 1969, "Kniga" Publishing House, Moscow, 1970, pp. 6-7. This annual statistical report on the book trade is hereafter referred to as the Pechat.

Republic Publishing Houses

In the larger Republics such as the Russian Soviet Federated Republic and the Ukrainian S.S.R. there are a great many publishing houses and a very large output of books and pamphlets, especially of elementary and secondary school textbooks.

In fact the combined output in copies of the publishing houses in the Russian Republic and the Ukraine - 571,290,000 copies in 1969 - was greater than the output of the Central or nationwide publishing houses.

An example of the organization and publishing in one of the smaller Republics - the Byelorussian S.S.R., which we visited, is given below.

Table 2

Book and Pamphlet Publishing in the Byelorussian S.S.R.
1969

	Number of Publishing Houses	Number of Titles	Number of Copies
Publishing Houses under the Republic Press Committee	7	856	22,309,000
Subject jointly to the Press Committee	2	199	782,000
Publishing by other organizations and institutions	Not Available	953	955,000
Total		2,008	24,046,000

Source: Table 43, _Pechat_ 1969

Control of Printing Plants

As in the case of publishing houses, a sizable number of book manufacturing plants are directly subject to the U.S.S.R. Press Committee. Others are under the control of the Republic Press Committees, ministries, and other organizations. Even some individual publishing houses, such as the U.S.S.R. Academy of Science, have their own printing facilities.

Organization of Book Distribution

The present organization of book distribution will be described in greater detail in Chapter IV, but at the top level it parallels the central control of book publishing. The Press Committee has a deputy in charge of the book and pamphlet sales organization Soyuzkniga. Similarly, the Republic Press Committees have a distribution section concerned primarily with distribution of the books published in those Republics. For nationwide distribution Soyuzkniga in Moscow deals directly with and ships to some 320 regional and local distribution organizations known as Knigotorgs.

Control of Paper

Since the supply of paper remained in 1970, as it was in 1962, the principal limiting factor on Soviet book production, the allocation of scarce paper supplies is one of the most important functions in the overall organization and control of Soviet book publishing. The U.S.S.R. Press Committee allocates paper to publishers for book and magazine production. Sub-allocations of Republic paper supplies for book and magazine production are also handled by Republic Press Committees for Publishing.

Title Control

The Book Chamber, subordinate to the State Committee, continues as in 1962 to exercise final clearance for publication of individual titles. Each book, with certain exceptions, such as books in foreign languages designed primarily for sale abroad, must have printed in it certain basic data. (See page 78 for an example.)

III. OPERATION OF A PUBLISHING HOUSE

Reports of British delegations who visited the U.S.S.R. after 1962 and our visits make it clear that the organization of individual publishing houses has remained essentially unchanged since 1962. No effort was made to obtain specific information on this point, but there is reason to wonder whether Party representatives and Trade Union representatives have recently achieved greater status and authority, for they were either present at our meetings, or given prominent mention.

The number of publishing houses has been reduced and the survivors are probably more efficient. On the few occasions when annual thematic plans were discussed, there seemed to be every indication that successful execution was quite common if not universal.

Profit incentives under the new economic plan* were being tested in six representative publishing houses. As a general consequence there was frequent presentation of facts such as total number of titles published, average printing, total printing, total authors' sheets and net sales results (for 1969). Margins are no longer the "modest profit" previously reported; the range commonly cited was from 20 to 25 percent of net sales.

Under the new economic plan the Soviet system of incentives in effect in 1962 is being superseded. The principal results of the new plan, when applied to an efficient, profitable publishing house, are quarterly cash bonuses plus additional benefits distributed on an annual basis. Prominent among the latter are permanent housing for staff members, holiday housing and subsidy of recreational and cultural activities. Some of the features of the earlier plan have also been retained but the direct benefits to the workers appears to be paramount. No detailed comparisons between old and new plans were offered or requested.

Again, there was no discussion of censorship. What conclusions in that regard can be drawn from the "identification" number on almost

---

*Subsequent to our visit, at the Communist Party Congress in the spring of 1971 most of the scheme for judging the performance of economic establishments on a monetary rather than a physical production basis seems to have been eliminated.

every book is open to challenge. Whether loss or lack of membership in the Writers' Union effectively denies creative authors access to formal publication could not be determined.

There were specific examples given of the use of press, radio and television to promote authors and their books. This effort appeared to be more thorough than the little more than announcement of availability previously reported. In general, relations between publishing houses and the distribution system seemed appropriately amicable, perhaps because publishers and their authors share losses from books remaining unsold.

The staffs of some publishing houses seemed either large or extraordinarily large in relation to titles published and other simple measures of work performed. The numbers of workers in U.S.S.R. publishing houses, which have little or no marketing program, and no warehouse, shipping and order fulfillment operations, are equal to similar American houses operating those services. Publishers who have yet to experience other than a "sellers" market may be able to support larger staffs.

The use of electronic data processing equipment is not available to the publishing houses, or even the two major distribution systems, Soyuzkniga and Mezh-Kniga. Management information systems are, therefore, not in use probably because controls over inventory and accounts receivable do not concern publishing houses.

Discussion of maintaining stock of titles making up a back list has no meaning in the U.S.S.R. where progress is measured by the number of copies _printed_, not _sold_.

IV.   BOOK DISTRIBUTION

The basic organizational arrangements for the distribution and sale of books in the U.S.S.R. remain essentially as described in our earlier report except for changes at the topmost levels. The principal book and pamphlet network, the All Union Book Trade Association (Soyuzkniga) is no longer subordinate to the Ministry of Culture but to the U.S.S.R. Press Committee. Similarly the Republic Press Committees control distribution of books published within their Republics.

For the big job of nationwide distribution - principally of books and pamphlets in the Russian language - Soyuzkniga in Moscow deals and ships directly to some 320 regional and local distribution centers known as Knigotorgs.

There are now approximately 14,500 shops selling books in the U.S.S.R. - 5,700 under Republic Press Committees; 7,650 in the consumer cooperative systems; and 1,150 under other ministries and organizations.

Improvements in Bookstores

We were struck by the greatly improved physical appearance and layout of several bookstores which we visited, especially a medical bookstore in Moscow and Dom Kniga (House of Books), also in Moscow, a three-year old establishment and the leading bookstore in the U.S.S.R. Both were new buildings, well lighted and attractively furnished. In Dom Kniga there were center counters and displays, and thus very much better access to books by the customer than in the old standard arrangement of ceiling-high shelves behind counters with clerks in between. Dom Kniga is a very large establishment with 5600 square meters of floor space and a staff of 211 sales people, 44,000 book and pamphlet titles in stock, and over 5,000,000 rubles a year in sales. The store is open seven days a week and serves 30,000 to 35,000 customers a day.

Other Developments

A number of other developments of the past eight years which deserve brief mention are:

1. A good deal of the shipping of books is now being done by truck, in contrast to the earlier almost exclusive reliance on rail transport. This is in line with the very considerable

improvement in the road network and the use of truck transport on a much larger scale for other materials as well.

2. Beginning in 1966 it became possible for publishers to print more books than Soyuzkniga agreed to purchase - in which case the excess printing by the publishers would not be paid for in advance but only if and when the distribution network succeeded in selling the books.

3. A point not covered in our earlier report concerns postal rates for books - significant because of the importance of mail order purchases for specialized books, especially by professional people living in remote areas. The special postage rate for books is set at half the regular rate for other packages; is a flat rate for the entire country; but is limited to packages of 1 kilogram or less.

V.   STATISTICS ON BOOK PRODUCTION AND PRICES

Adoption by the U.S.S.R. of the 1964 UNESCO recommendation on standardized publishing statistics has resulted in much more meaningful data on books and pamphlets in the recent issues of the statistical yearbook on publishing: Pechat' S.S.S.R. Especially helpful is the provision of separate figures for book and pamphlet output (books being 49 pages or more); the separation of original and revised editions from straight reprintings; and more detail in reporting data on publications sold through the book trade and those given away free.

Thus, of the four difficulties in comparing Soviet production with that of the U.S.A. listed in our 1962 report (pages 92-93) only two major problems remain:

1. The fact that each translated edition of the same book title into the numerous languages used in the U.S.S.R. counts as a separate title, which inflates the title output of the U.S.S.R. as compared with countries with a single language; and

2. The U.S. failure to collect and publish data on book production by federal, state and local governments.

Soviet Book Production 1961-1969

Comparison of Soviet book production in 1961 with 1969 (the latest year for which published statistics are available) cannot, unfortunately, deal separately with books and pamphlets, nor original editions and reprint editions, since this data was not available in 1961. Thus, the comparison will have to be made for books and pamphlets combined, with some help from a comparison of priced books and pamphlets as distinguished from those given away, which are predominantly pamphlets. The table below gives some of the basic 1961 and 1969 data on book and pamphlet production.

14

Table 3

U.S.S.R. Combined Book and Pamphlet Production, 1961 and 1969

	1961	1969	Percentage Change
Unpriced Publications			
Titles	24,476	23,218	-5%
Copies	77,500,000	76,587,000	-1%
Priced Publications			
Titles	49,523	51,369	+ 4%
Copies	1,031,900,000	1,239,134,000	+ 20%
Value (rubles)	376,500,000	530,068,000	+ 41%
Average price per copy	36 kopecks	43 kopecks	+ 17%
Copies per capita	5.2	5.2	0
Combined, Priced and Unpriced			
Titles	73,999	74,587	+ 1%
Copies	1,119,400,000	1,315,721,000	+ 18%
Copies per capita	5.55	5.48	0

Sources: _Pechat_, 1961, 1969

As shown in Table 3 above, the following are the principal differences between 1961 and 1969 with respect to the overall output of books and pamphlets:

Total combined production has increased 1 percent in titles, and 18 percent in number of copies, with no change in copies per capita. Production of unpriced publications has declined both in number of titles and number of copies.

Production of priced publications has

increased 4 percent in number of titles

increased 20 percent in number of copies

increased 40 percent in total value

increased 17 percent in average price per title.

On a per capita basis there has been little change in the last eight years - a slight (6%) increase in total book and pamphlet copies per capita and a stable level of 5.2 copies per capita for priced books and pamphlets.

Comparison of Books and Pamphlets, New Editions and Reprints

Since 1961 figures are not available on the breakdown between books and pamphlets and between original editions and straight reprints of existing books, no comparison between 1961 and 1969 can be made in these areas. The table below for the year 1969 shows what information is available in the Pechat on these two points.

Table 4

U.S.S.R. Production 1969:*

Books, pamphlets, original
editions and reprint editions

	Books	Pamphlets	Books and Pamphlets
New editions			
Titles			67,673
Number of copies	Not Available	Not Available	745,610,000
Reprints			
Titles			6,914
Number of copies	Not Available	Not Available	570,111,000
Total			
Titles	41,317	33,270	74,587
Number of copies	921,191,000	394,530,000	1,315,721,000
Number of copies per capita	3.8	1.7	5.5

****

(Copies per capita of books in U.S.A., 1969)

	Books	Pamphlets	Books and Pamphlets
U.S. Population 1969	203,213,000	Not Available	Not Available
Copies of books sold	1,435,000,000	Not Available	Not Available
Number of copies per capita	7.1	Not Available	Not Available

* Source: Pechat, 1969

It will be noted that the number of copies per capita for books of 49 or more pages produced in the U.S.S.R. was 3.8 in 1969. This compares with an estimated sale of 7.1 books per capita (production figures not being collected) in the U.S.A. in 1969, not including publications of federal, state and local governments.

16

VI.   FOREIGN TRADE

There seems to have been no significant change in the last few years in the organization of foreign trade in books, publications and related materials. Mezhdunarodnaia Kniga (Mezh-Kniga) in the Ministry of Foreign Trade still has the responsibility for these activities, both on the export and import side.

Volume and Distribution in Foreign Trade

An examination of official foreign trade statistics shows very little difference in the volume of imports and exports in books and other publications in 1968 and 1969 as compared with 1960 and 1961, the figures cited in tables 7-10 in our 1962 report. Import and export volumes were approximately the same in the two periods, with much the largest quantity of foreign trade being done with the Eastern European Socialist countries. Both imports from and exports to the U.S. and Western European countries remained minimal. In printing equipment, however, (see Appendix F) the volume of imports doubled from 1960 and 1961 to 1968 and 1969, with most of the increase being from the countries of Western Europe. East Germany remained, however, the largest single source of imported printing equipment for the Soviet Union.

17

VII. BOOK MANUFACTURING IN THE U.S.S.R.

The Delegation visited two major printing plants during its visit: The Byelorussian Printing Works, built in Minsk in 1953, and the Ivan Fyorodov Printing House in Leningrad, established in the 1890's for the purpose of producing works of high quality. The impression resulting from both visits was that the general composition of the work force and the conditions of work were similar to those observed in 1962, but there was a noticeable upgrading of equipment quality. In Minsk, a general purpose plant printing in the Byelorussian, Russian, German, English, and French languages, the equipment was primarily of Soviet manufacture, although East German offset equipment (including four-color) was in evidence, and new photocomposition machinery and better offset presses were on order for installation in 1971 "for improved textbooks." Over half the production of the Minsk plant was for other Republics of the Soviet Union, and the engineering staff directors were graduates of the Moscow or Ivov Printers Colleges. As in other State enterprises the employees (1442 in number, 70% of them women, with 1392 directly involved in manufacturing) enjoyed bonus benefits and plant-operated nurseries, kindergartens, pioneers' camps, and rest homes.

The Leningrad plant continues on its initial mission of producing high quality work, and still employs much careful hand work in its letterpress, intaglio, offset and binding processes. A staff of 800 produces about 1,400,000 books per year, the majority art books for Leningrad publishers as well as other Soviet houses (plus some work for Czechoslovakia and other bloc countries placed through Soviet intermediaries). Here again, much of the most modern equipment - four color offset perfector and a 36-pocket collator - was from East Germany, and in this particular case had been display units exhibited at the most recent Moscow printing machinery fair. The books produced, including reproductions of works from the Hermitage and photographs of Leningrad monuments, were well-designed, well-made, and extremely attractive.

VIII.   BELLES LETTRES

The term <u>Belles Lettres</u> as used in this report includes poetry, fiction and literary criticism. The same publishing houses in the U.S.S.R. issue all three. Of the publishing houses we visited, Progress, Khudozhestvennaya Literatura and the Writers Union were the most concerned with creative writing.

Progress publishes in the Russian language books from other countries that have appeared within the last five to ten years. While we were there, we were told John Cheever's <u>Bullet Park</u> and John O'Hara's <u>The Instrument</u> were being published. The Editor-in-Chief, Torsuyev, was extremely critical of <u>Portnoy's Complaint</u>, we believe for moral reasons. While it was hard to be sure of meanings in translation, we believe it was the editor's feeling that the only reason that <u>Portnoy</u> had been published was profit.

Progress employs over 1000 people; they publish over 600 titles translated from the Russian into about 35 languages. About 130 foreign titles are translated into Russian. World publications are studied through catalogues in the Foreign Language Library in Moscow. Editors are assigned by language and subject. English is the largest section. About 15 American books are translated into Russian annually.

The Khudozhestvennaya Literatura Publishing House publishes classics of artistic literature, both from Russian and the peoples of the U.S.S.R. and from foreign lands. As many as 381 titles, totaling 88,346,000 copies were published by this publishing house in 1970.

At the Writers Union our visit was short and full of facts and figures. There are 7,000 members, and the Union publishes many books and magazines--but no discussion in depth of what is published, from where does it come, and how are publishing decisions made, occurred.

No in-depth picture of the content of the current output of fiction, belles lettres and poetry was secured by our delegation. This would have taken weeks more than we were able to devote to the matter, and a command of the Russian language. We would also have to have reached a state of frankness which is difficult in large group discussions and in discussions where the parties are meeting for the first time.

For example, we did not discuss the whole relationship of the government to the publisher and how this affects the creativity of the author and the decision making powers of the publisher. Censorship was not discussed. How does it work? Who are the censors? What is their background? Is there an appeal from their decision--by whom, to whom?

If we were to try and publish more books from the U.S.S.R. here, what orderly procedures could be established? How can we get notification of publication of American books in the U.S.S.R. even though royalties are not to be paid? What authors have been paid when they requested monies and appeared in the U.S.S.R.?

We learned more about how the system for fiction publishing in the U.S.S.R. works by reading what we could about the struggles of authors critical of the government in the press than we did in our official discussions. More talk and more publishing is needed in this area. It should be on a continual basis and we hope it can be arranged. It is desperately needed if our two nations are to get a better understanding of each other.

IX. SCIENTIFIC AND TECHNICAL BOOKS

The reorganization of book publishing, printing and distribution in 1964 has been described in Chapter II. Some of the consolidations which were then made affected scientific and technical publishing houses.

Nauka, the Publishing House of the U.S.S.R. Academy of Sciences, now includes the programs formerly the responsibility of the Publishing House for Far Eastern Literature and the State Publishing House of Literature for Physics and Mathematics (Fizmatgiz). Thus, the term "science" even more than before means every academic subject, including humanities and classics. Nauka, certainly the largest and most comprehensive publishing house in the U.S.S.R., may also be one of the largest in the world. It remains, together with printing plants and bookstores, under the control of the Academy. Sales of journals and books in 1969 were approximately 24 million rubles resulting in a profit of 2.2 million rubles.

Among the major publishing programs are:

1. Literary classics, literary criticism and commentaries with printings of 50 to 300 thousand copies per title.
2. Specialized monographs for which printings are very small, sometimes only a few hundred but usually from 1,000 to 2,000 copies.
3. Basic textbooks in physics and mathematics requiring printings and reprintings as large as 100,000 copies.
4. Scientific journals of which 46 are translated into English, 6 under contractual agreement with an American publisher.

Virtually all of the publications of Nauka are original works by authors in the U.S.S.R. although occasionally a foreign author's work will be accepted. They estimate about one third of all of their publications are translated into foreign languages including about 100 books a year which Nauka itself translates and publishes in foreign languages.

In response to a question about areas of science of current interest, Nauka reported publishing about 20 titles each year on computers and data processing, and a few titles on information science.

No publications are available in the form of microfilm, microfiche, computer tape or computer printouts.

Mir is the successor to The State Publishing House for Foreign Literature and The Publishing House of Foreign Languages. The result is a very large publishing house which is responsible for translation of foreign books and journals into Russian, and for translation of Russian books into foreign (non-U.S.S.R.) languages. A notable addition to Mir's program is science fiction with printings of from 100-200 thousand copies in Russian language editions and 30-50 thousand copies in foreign languages.

Although visits were made only to Nauka and Mir, visits to bookstores specializing in scientific and technical books, and medical books provided opportunities to examine translations of American books which were reported very much in demand. There is also much useful additional information in the reports of the 1964, 1966 and 1970 British delegations.

There have been reports from time to time that American technical and scientific journals are reproduced in offset editions in the U.S.S.R. This is a fact, since we found many examples in the reference sections of the library of the Byelorussian Academy of Sciences in Minsk. It was not possible during the remaining days of our trip to find and to visit the organization responsible for this program, nor was it possible to determine whether similar offset editions of books are also produced.

X. TEXTBOOKS FOR ELEMENTARY AND SECONDARY SCHOOLS

The largest publishing house specializing in student texts, pedagogical texts, and teaching aids, is Prosveschcheniye, formed in 1964 through merging of the publishing arm of the Academy of Pedagogical Sciences and other similarly oriented enterprises. A staff of 700, of which 500 are in Moscow and the remainder in Leningrad, deals through its 22 sections with teachers, 2,500 writers, institutes, boards, school officials, and some 40 printers to produce over 250 million books per year, four-fifths of them texts for the eight compulsory years of schooling (which is to be raised to ten).

Prosveschcheniye is an All-Union house, issuing its books in Russian and other Soviet languages, as well as in German, English, French, and other languages studied in the schools. Foreign language teaching is often begun in the second grade. Pedagogical evaluation and analysis are carried on over a two- to three-year period after the text plan has been adopted by the Educational Collegium, and on the average a set of textbooks is expected to be used for at least five years in the classroom.

No programmed learning books are yet being issued, and computer-assisted instruction is only in the experimental stage, but some audio-visual aid texts are provided for issuance elsewhere as tapes, slides, films, etc. A special department for the handicapped publishes (only in Russian) for blind, poorly sighted, deaf, or hearing impaired students. In Braille alone, some 350 books are published (for adults as well as for children) and include fiction as well as classroom texts.

Royalties for authors follow standard patterns with an additional bonus of double royalty if a work is plated and not revised during the five years of its use. The house's profits, which are considerable, are being invested in a Crimean sanatorium to accommodate 200 vacationing staff, a Baltic boarding house, a Pioneers camp, employees' club on the firm's premises, and Moscow apartment houses.

23

XI. CHILDREN'S BOOKS

We visited one publisher of children's books, Detskaya Literatura Publishing House. Again we will not repeat figures and description given in the 1962 report. The interest and devotion of the staff people we spoke to was unusual. The quality of the books ranged all the way from very simple and inexpensive, to really superb in both illustration and binding. Literary quality we were unable to determine. However, children's publishing seems to be flourishing.

The production of children's books in the U.S.S.R. in 1969 was over 270.4 million copies.

Detskaya publishes over 650 titles a year for children 3 to 17 years old. What we refer to as "flats" are the most popular and from what we saw deservedly so. Besides Detskaya there are 89 other publishers in the U.S.S.R. producing children's books in over 70 languages; some printings go as high as 1.5 million. About 50% go to schools and libraries. The rest are sold to individuals. On the average 10% of the total volume is exported.

Of the 650 titles published by Detskaya in 1969, 250 to 300 were new books while the rest were reprints. The demand for all books, with the possible exception of political tracts, exceed the supply in the Soviet Union. Some of the children's books published by Detskaya are translated into English, French, German and other languages by Progress. A special library for authors and others interested in children's books is maintained and has over 200,000 volumes. Connected with the children's literature publishing house there is a research house (Children's Book House) with a staff of approximately 50 persons. This house arranges for groups of children in Moscow to meet with authors and publishers to exchange ideas. It arranges for exhibits and lectures for librarians and teachers. Approximately 200 children per day from the Moscow schools are invited to the research house. Seminars are organized for teachers twice a month at which authors speak. From what we could gather, the research center is for both instruction and to get a feeling of the ideas of what kind of books students and teachers would like to see done. There are four such research centers in the Soviet Union, the others being in Leningrad, Tbilisi and Kiev. The Moscow center also works to publicize children's books on radio and television.

If a system could be established for American publishers to look at Soviet books and vice versa, some business could be done here with a saving to both countries in using color plates of the other country.

XII.   TEXTBOOKS FOR HIGHER EDUCATION
(Moscow State University Press)

Time did not permit our visiting a publishing house which concentrated on higher education texts, but we did pay a call on Moscow State University Press. This press, with a publishing staff of 150 and a printing staff of 400, issues annually 400 new books or revised editions in editions from 500 to 150,000 copies. The books come from all faculties of Moscow State University (with some exceptions, e.g., agriculture, medicine) and are chosen within the faculties themselves. The main purpose of the Press is to produce monographs, and works are issued in French, German, Spanish, and Oriental languages as well as in Russian. Like other publishers, it prepares an annual statistical plan and has its own budget, though it is a department of the University. The annual receipts from sales amount to one million rubles, and the profit (as in many other houses) is in the 20% range. In addition to monographs, the Press publishes a number of textbooks for use at the University, as well as sixteen series of journals with circulation of 3,000-4,000 copies. In some instances, authors are invited to write on a specific subject, and the Press also produces multi-authored works such as conference proceedings.

Nearly all major universities in the Republics have their own presses, but there is little, if any, interchange of information among them. In Minsk, for example, the Byelorussian University is establishing a press, a result of discussion between the Ministry of Higher Education and the Republic Press Committee, with apparently no exchange of information about other similar publishing houses elsewhere in the U.S.S.R.

XIII. ENCYCLOPEDIA AND DICTIONARY PUBLISHING

For over forty years the Soviet Encyclopedia Publishing House has been publishing encyclopedias and dictionaries intended for a wide circle of users.

The information on the publication of encyclopedias has been drawn principally from a conference at the Soviet Encyclopedia Publishing House of the U.S.S.R. in Moscow. This publishing house was reorganized into its present form as a publisher of the Great Soviet Encyclopedia, dictionaries, special purpose encyclopedias and reference books in 1966 following the general reorganization of U.S.S.R. publishing. It operates under the U.S.S.R. Press Committee and in conjunction with its predecessor houses has published more than ninety universal and specialized encyclopedic editions.

After the completion of the second edition of the Great Soviet Encyclopedia the publishing house issued the Small Soviet Encyclopedia, the Encyclopedia Dictionary, specialized encyclopedias, such as those of physics, chemistry, medicine, geography, economics. The encyclopedias of history, philosophy, literature, theatre and others will soon come off the press.

The Publishing House is now preparing the third edition of the Great Soviet Encyclopedia in thirty volumes. (The second edition was published in 1949-1959 in fifty-one volumes plus an index of two volumes.) The page size of the third edition will be slightly larger than of the second and the format of the page will be in three columns rather than two as in the previous edition. Also, the type size will be eight point while the second edition was printed in seven point type. A number of the articles of the second edition have been pruned down for the third edition.

Volumes #1 through #3 of the third edition of the Great Soviet Encyclopedia already have been published with four or five additional volumes to be published each year and the set finally completed by 1976. The new third edition will have approximately 30,000 pages with 100,000 articles and will contain approximately 40,000 illustrations, 17,000 maps and more than 20,000 biographies. An index in either one or two volumes probably will be provided for the thirty volume set at a later date.

Brochures announcing the third edition of the Great Soviet Encyclopedia were mailed to book stores in 1969. In two and a half months, 600,000 orders were received and it was necessary to close out the sale in April of 1970 as no more paper was available to print a greater number of sets   (300,000 copies of the second edition of the Great Soviet Encyclopedia were published and sold). The price per volume is five and a half rubles, making the price for the total set - exclusive of index - one hundred and sixty-five rubles.

The sale of encyclopedias in the Soviet Union is conducted entirely through book stores. No door-to-door salespeople are involved in the selling process.

An annual supplement to the encyclopedia has been published each year since 1957 containing approximately 600 pages and priced at four rubles per volume.

This publishing house has 180 full time editors and a total of 450 members on the staff. In addition, the first volume of the third edition involved 1,100 outside authors for its completion. The additional volumes will involve many other outside authors with the total number helping in the over-all project estimated at probably 15,000 total.

All of the multi-volume works are published one volume at a time over a period of months or years and are subscribed to in advance. This contrasts with the current American practice of publishing multi-volume encyclopedias in complete sets.

In the last four years this publishing house also has brought out other encyclopedias as follows:

Multi-volume

Philosophic Encyclopedia, vols. 1-5

Economic Life of the U.S.S.R. Chronicle of Events and Facts. 1917-1965. In 2 volumes.

Teachers' Encyclopedia, vols. 1-4

Physical Encyclopedic Dictionary, vols. 1-5

Concise Chemical Encyclopedia, vols. 1-5

Concise Geographic Encyclopedia, vols. 1-5

Small Medical Encyclopedia, vols. 1-12

Theatrical Encyclopedia, vols. 1-5

Motion Picture Dictionary, vols. 1-2

Single-volume

Labor Law Encyclopedic Dictionary, 3rd edition

Encyclopedic Dictionary of Geographic Terms

Large Medical Encyclopedia Yearbook, I, II

Popular Medical Encyclopedia, 5th, 6th, 7th editions

Automobile. Maintenance and Repair. Encyclopedic Dictionary-Reference Books

The "Small Encyclopedias" series

Great October Socialist Revolution

Cosmonauts. 1st, 2nd editions

Quantum Electronics

The Olympic Games

Atomic Energy

Miscellaneous

Encyclopedic Dictionary "Union of Soviet Republics. 1917-1967"

Encyclopedic Music Dictionary in 1 volume

"Automation of Production and Industrial Electronics" in 4 volumes

"Construction Materials" in 3 volumes

Economic Encyclopedia "Industry and Construction" in 3 volumes, and others.

The publishing house intends to publish a music encyclopedia in 5 volumes.

"Political Economy" Encyclopedia

Polytechnical Dictionary

Mathematics Encyclopedia in 3 volumes

"Polimery" Encyclopedic Dictionary in 3 volumes, and others.

In addition to encyclopedias of nationwide significance, a family of local Soviet encyclopedias is in being or in preparation. Each of the republics of the U.S.S.R. is in the process of producing its own encyclopedia in its native tongue. All of these encyclopedias (with the exception of the Daghesten Encyclopedia, which will be published in Russian) will be published in national languages.

The most important of these encyclopedias are:

1. Ukrainian Soviet Encyclopedia, in 17 volumes, vols. 1-17 plus Kiev Index, 1959-1965 (1968 Index), nearly 50,000 articles, printed in 80,000-100,000 copies, price--3 rubles per volume.

2. Ukrainian Soviet Encyclopedic Dictionary, in 3 volumes, vols. 1-3, Kiev, 1966-1968, 40,000 articles, 75,000 copies, price--3 rubles per volume.

3. Ukrainian Soviet Socialist Republic, translated from Ukrainian, Kiev, 1967, 50,000 copies, price--3 rubles per volume (Russian translation of 17th volume of the Ukrainian Soviet Encyclopedia).

4. Encyclopedia of the National Economy of the Ukrainian S.S.R., in 4 volumes, vol. 1, Kiev, 1969, printing of 30,000 copies, price--3 rubles 25 kopecks per volume (there will be 4,000 articles in the complete publication).

5. Small Encyclopedia of the Latvian S.S.R., in 3 volumes, vols. 1-3, Riga, 1967-1970, 12,000 articles, 50,000 copies, price--5 rubles per volume.

6. Agricultural Encyclopedia, in 4 volumes, vols. 1-3, Riga, 1962-1966, printing of 13,000 copies, price--3 rubles 96 kopecks per volume (in the Latvian language).

7. Small Lithuanian Soviet Encyclopedia, in 3 volumes, vols. 1-2, Vilnius, 1966-1968, 60,000 copies, price--5 rubles, 25,000 words (in the complete publication).

8. Byelorussian Soviet Encyclopedia, in 12 volumes, vols. 1-2, Minsk, 1969-1970, 25,000 copies, 45,000 articles (in the complete publication), price--2 rubles 50 kopecks.

9. Estonian Soviet Encyclopedia, in 8 volumes, vols. 1-2, Tallin, 1968-1970, 65,000 copies, 50,000 articles (in the complete publication), price--4 rubles 50 kopecks.

10. Moldavian Soviet Encyclopedia, in 8 volumes, vol. 1, Kishinev, 1970, 40,000 articles (in the complete publication), price--4 rubles 75 kopecks. Printing of 40,000 copies.

The first volumes of republican encyclopedias in Azerbaijan, Armenia, Georgia, Kazakhstan, Turkmenia, and Uzbekistan are expected to be published in the near future.

The first volume of a new Byelorussian Soviet Encyclopedia in twelve volumes has just been published by Minsk. Two volumes per year are planned with completion of the entire twelve volumes in about five years. The publication will contain approximately 40,000 entries, 7,500 pages with the emphasis on the Republic of Byelorussia. Each volume will contain fifteen pages in full color with additional black and white illustrations totalling approximately 10,000 in the completed set. The Republic of Byelorussia has donated a new, modern design, four story building to house the editors and staff for the publication of Byelorussian Soviet Encyclopedia.

XIV.   TRANSLATIONS

Visits were made to three publishing houses with major or principal interests in translations. A.P.N., founded in 1964, is the publishing arm of the Novosti Press Agency. Mir and Progress are the result of consolidations which occurred when the State Committee was established in 1964.

A.P.N.

A.P.N. is partly a propaganda activity, and partly a literary agency. It publishes books and pamphlets in English, French, German, Spanish, Chinese, Vietnamese and other languages, to describe and explain the U.S.S.R. and its domestic and foreign policies. A magazine, Sputnik, published in Russian, English, French and German is modeled after Readers Digest. A major effort is to seek and accept commissions for authoritative manuscripts in English or other important languages, with a guaranty that there will be no prior publication in any language in the U.S.S.R. Western publishers, including some in the United States, use this route for obtaining valid international copy-right. Various agreements can be reached including world rights to more than one language. A.P.N. reported selling about one hundred manuscripts a year, sometimes with additional separate charge for illustrations. Novosti continues to supply separately to foreign publishers illustrative materials, especially photographs, subject to an understanding that nothing will be used to denigrate the U.S.S.R.

Mir is the Russian word for "peace," and Peace is the English imprint used for books in that language. This house is a result of the consolidation of those parts of the Publishing House of Foreign Literature which was responsible for scientific and technical books, and equivalent parts of The Publishing House of Foreign Languages (see Progress below). Mir translates about 200 titles each year into Russian with total printings of several millions, and about half that number into foreign languages with total printings exceeding one million copies. The average printing of translated books is about 15,000 copies, the exception being science fiction for which printings are from 800,000 to one million copies. Mir has continued the New Books

<u>Abroad</u>, a monthly periodical complete with recommendations for and against translation. Finally, Mir is still responsible for translations into Russian of some scientific and technical journals.

Progress, the other consolidation referred to above, is a successor to The Publishing House of Foreign Languages as well as a few lesser parts of The Publishing House of Foreign Literature. The primary objective is to translate Russian books (other than technical, scientific and professional) into thirty different languages; books from foreign languages are also translated. Although English and other European languages are predominant in the program some books are published in Arabic and in African languages such as Swahili and Hausa. Journals are published in Russian and foreign languages. Progress specializes in the humanities, fiction, history, economics, textbooks for foreigners to learn Russian and a few books in the sciences such as geography.

In 1970 Progress published a new definitive 45 volume anniversary edition of Lenin's Collected Works in English, French and Finnish. Titles in the current catalog are about 30 percent Marx, Engels and Lenin, 25 percent fiction including juveniles and 8 percent textbooks. Two-thirds are in foreign languages. Typically about fifteen American titles, usually fiction, are translated each year. Printings of books in Russian are from ten to twenty thousand copies but it is difficult to obtain printing sizes on books published for export.

Foreign books are also translated and published by specialized publishing houses such as that for nursing and medicine. Foreign journals urgently needed are available in editions printed by offset from the originals, and this method is probably being used in lieu of translation for more specialized journals. The journals in wide demand continue to be translated.

XV. AUTHORS' ROYALTIES

Authors' royalties are determined by decrees of the Councils of Ministers of the several Republics, the most important of which is the Russian Republic, in which book publishing is concentrated. The basic decrees of the RSFSR in this field remain No. 530 of April 7, 1960, for belles lettres, and No. 326 of March 20, 1962, for political, scientific, technical, education and other literature which were described in our earlier report.

Standard Author's Contract

A standard or model publisher-author agreement, or publishing contract, was issued on April 10, 1967, by the Chairman of the Press Committee pursuant to a directive of the Council of Ministers of the U.S.S.R. of February 16, 1967. The model contract is in two forms, one dealing with literary and artistic works, and the other with political, scientific, technical, scholarly and other works, but they are virtually identical. Each of the Republic Press Committees is required to apply the same standards for publishing organizations under their jurisdictions. This model contract is of sufficient interest to justify its inclusion in English translation in full in Appendix C to this report.

XVI.   COPYRIGHT

As in 1962 we raised the question of the U.S.S.R. coming into one of the international copyright conventions on every appropriate occasion. We had particularly detailed discussions with the Chairman of the State Committee for Publishing, Mr. Stukalin; at the Writers' Union; at the Mezhdunarodnaia Kniga. In contrast to our 1962 experience we found no hesitancy about discussing the pros and cons in a perfectly objective way, with a good understanding of the two conventions on the part of the key Soviet officials. Some individuals, speaking personally, said they favored entry of the U.S.S.R. into one of the conventions; other individuals said they expected that such a development would come in time; and a leading official of the Writers' Union said that his organization was on record as advocating this course of action.

Changes in Copyright Law and Regulations

Soviet copyright law and regulations remain essentially those described in our earlier report, However, since 1962 the U.S.S.R. and Hungary have adopted a bilateral copyright agreement giving somewhat restricted reciprocal copyright protection to nationals of the other country.

The basic structure of Soviet copyright law is covered in translation in Appendix B to this report.

The Case for International Copyright

Explaining the advantages to the U.S.S.R. and its authors, as well as the authors' publishers and readers of the rest of the world, our delegation essentially repeated the case which is set forth in great detail in Chapter XVI of our earlier report. We pointed out, however, that developments since 1962 had, in our view, strengthened this case, especially in the following respects:

1.   The U.S.S.R. domestic copyright term of the life of the author and 15 years is, in most cases, a longer term than the minimum of 25 years from date of publication in the Universal Copyright Convention; although still short of the Berne Union term of life plus 50 years.

2. In the period 1962-68 Soviet book production had remained relatively static, barely matching the growth of population, although the average per unit price of a book had increased significantly. In contrast, book production in the U.S. and other Western countries, measured in number of copies, had increased enormously in the past eight years, and because of almost universal inflation, prices had also increased very substantially. Therefore, we felt that if in 1962 the Soviet Union would more than break even in terms of hard currency acquisition versus hard currency outlay, we believe that these comparative developments in publishing in the U.S.S.R. and the West increased the potential market for Soviet works in the rest of the world more substantially than the growth of the Soviet market for Western works. Therefore we felt that the economic case which we had made in 1962 had been strengthened by developments in the intervening years.

3. Similarly, the growth of international trade in books, especially scientific, technical and professional books, had increased greatly in the rest of the world since 1962, as had the ability of major companies, especially in the U.S., to market this type of book through a worldwide distribution network. There had been no similar growth in the ability of Mezhdunarodnaia Kniga to market its books abroad. Therefore, this factor contributed a further potential increase in the market for Soviet books in translation in the world languages such as English, French, German and Spanish.

When this case was made in our final meeting on November 3, Chairman Stukalin of the State Committee responded with a most penetrating question. To paraphrase, he said: Why, if joining an international copyright convention would be so much to the advantage of the U.S.S.R., are you as United States publishers urging such a course of action upon us?

36

Our reply was essentially twofold:

1. The amounts of money involved in the payment of copyright royalties are for both the U.S. and the U.S.S.R., as countries, infinitesimal - a few million dollars at most as compared with the tens of billions of dollars involved in the total balance of payments of both countries.

2. So far as the U.S. book publishers are concerned, we are used to paying royalties for rights to publish; we believe in paying royalties; and we are delighted to do so if as a result we get a book that is worth publishing and hopefully will produce a modest profit.

Our delegation expressed the hope that the Soviet agencies concerned would continue to study this question and be prepared to resume our discussions when the U.S.S.R. delegation made its return visit to the U.S.A. in 1971. Meanwhile, we undertook to prepare such estimates as might prove feasible as to what the volume of royalties might be from the U.S. and possibly other countries if the U.S.S.R. should come into an international copyright agreement; and to have these estimates ready for discussion when the U.S.S.R. delegation to the United States arrived in 1971. We suggested also that the U.S.S.R. might wish to have an observer delegation at the scheduled July 1971 diplomatic conferences in Paris to revise the Universal Copyright Convention and the Berne Convention.

To summarize, our delegation felt that progress was being made in the rational discussion of the advantages and disadvantages to the U.S.S.R. and other countries of having the Soviet Union undertake international copyright obligations on a multilateral basis. We reiterated our strong opinion that in the world languages bilateral arrangements were just not workable. We had the impression that a considerable number of technical problems of adjusting U.S.S.R. law and practice remained to be ironed out, but the two main questions in the minds of Soviet officials were:

First, and by all odds the most important - what would be the effect on the U.S.S.R.'s balance of payments in hard currency;

37

<u>Second</u> - to what extent would acceptance of international copyright obligations curtail the access of the U.S.S.R. to Western technology because Western publishers and authors might withhold permissions on ideological grounds or set translation fees to U.S.S.R. publishing houses at unreasonable levels. (Here we pointed out that the practice with respect to other countries indicated that Western publishers granted permissions on a reasonable basis and that the U.S.S.R. publishing house, being a monopoly buyer, would be in a strong bargaining position with the competitive publishing houses of the West).

We hope to continue these discussions and to make further progress on the basis of additional facts in our meetings with the U.S.S.R. delegation in the United States in 1971.

SCALE OF AUTHOR'S ROYALTIES FOR BELLES LETTRES
IN THE
RUSSIAN SOVIET FEDERATED SOCIALIST REPUBLIC

Taken from regulation No. 530, dated April 7, 1960, of the Council of Ministers of the Russian Soviet Federated Socialist Republic entitled: Author's Royalties for Belles Lettres.

In order to standardize author's royalties paid for publications of belles lettres, the Council of Ministers decrees:

I. Establishment of the following rates for author's royalties*

Kinds of Literature	Number of copies in thousands	Royalty rates per signature, 40 thousand characters (in rubles)	Lump-sum royalty rates for whole works (in rubles)
		Regular publications	
1. Prose	15	150; 225; 300; 400	--
2. Stories up to one signature long	--	--	150; 200; 250; 300; 400
3. One-act plays	--	--	200--600
4. Recordings of creative prose works	20	100; 125; 150; 175; 200	--
5. Poetry, per line	10	0,7; 1,2; 1,4; 1,7; 2,0	--
6. Verses up to 30 lines long and lyrics of any length	--	--	30; 60; 100; 150; 200
7. Epigrams and text for posters	--	--	10--60
8. Recordings of creative works in verse, per line	10	0,5; 0,8; 1,0; 1,2; 1,4	--
9. Pre-school and lower-grade children's publications (prose up to 1 signature, verse up to 100 lines)	50	--	150; 200; 250; 300; 400
10. Children's versions of belles lettres a) not exceeding 1 signature	50	--	75; 100; 125; 150; 200
b) more than 1 signature	20	75; 100; 125; 150; 200	--

*In new rubles

Kinds of Literature	Number of copies in thousands	Royalty rates per signature 40 thousand characters (in rubles)	Lump-sum royalty rates for whole works (in rubles)
11. Popular science literature for children	50	150; 200; 250; 300	--
12. Collected subject and encyclopedic books for children	--	20--80	--
13. Works of literary criticism, history and art	10	150; 225; 300; 400	--
14. Literary reviews (up to 0.5 signature)	--	--	100; 125; 150; 175; 200
15. Original bibliographies, annotations, calendars of meetings, annals and indexes	--	120--200	--
16. Translations: a) prose	15	50; 70; 100; 125; 150	--
b) poetry, per line	10	0,4; 0,7; 0,9; 1,1; 1,4	--
c) lyrics	--	--	30; 40; 60; 80; 100
17. Chrestomathics of belles lettres	--	30--80	--
18. Collections of literary materials: a) with textual analysis	--	20--60	--
b) without textual analysis	--	5--40	--
19. Collections of proverbs, sayings and catchwords	--	50--150	--
20. Commentaries and notes	--	50--200	--
21. Introductory articles, prefaces and epilogues	--	200--600	--

Kinds of Literature	Number of copies in thousands	Royalty rates per signature, 40 thousand characters (in rubles)	Lump-sum royalty rates for whole works (in rubles)
	Popular publications		
22. Prose	50--100	250; 300; 400	--
23. Recordings of creative prose works	50--100	150; 200	--
24. Poetry, per line	25--50	1,4; 1,7; 2,0	--
25. Recordings of creative works in verse, per line	25--50	1,0; 1,4	--
26. Children's versions of belles lettres a) not exceeding 1 signature	100--150	--	100; 150; 200
b) more than 1 signature	100--150	100; 150; 200	--
27. Works of literary criticism, history and art	25--50	250; 300; 400	--
28. Pre-school and lower-grade children's publications (prose up to 1 signature, verse up to 100 lines)	150	--	200; 300; 400
29. Popular science literature for children	100--150	200; 250; 300	--
30. Pre-school and lower-grade children's publications: a) prose	100--150	250; 300; 400	--
b) poetry, per line	100--150	1,4; 1,7; 2,0	--
31. Books in the series "School Library" a) prose	100--150	250; 300; 400	--
b) poetry, per line	100--150	1,4; 1,7; 2,0	--
32. Translations: a) prose	50--100	100; 125; 150	--
b) poetry, per line	25--50	0,9; 1,1; 1,4	--

Rates of author's royalties for items 2, 3, 6, 7, 12, 14, 15, 16 (b), 17, 18, 19, 20 and 21 are not related to the number of copies.

SUMMARY OF U.S.S.R. COPYRIGHT PROVISIONS

Taken from the basic Civil Code of the U.S.S.R. and Soviet Republics*

Article 96. Works covered by copyright.

Copyright is available for scientific, literary or artistic works, regardless of form, purpose or value of the work or of the means of its production.

Copyright is available for works whether published or not, if expressed in some objective form allowing for use of the creative work of the author (manuscript, sketch, drawing, public presentation, film, mechanical or magnetic tape, etc.).

Article 97. Copyright for works published in the U.S.S.R. and abroad.

Copyright for works first published in the U.S.S.R. or not published but located in the U.S.S.R. in some objective form, is recognized for the author and his descendants regardless of their citizenship.

Copyright is also recognized for citizens of the U.S.S.R. and their descendants whose works are first published or are located in some objective form in a foreign country.

Copyright for other persons for works first published or located in some objective form in a foreign country is recognized only on the basis of and within corresponding international agreements concluded by the U.S.S.R.

Article 98. Rights of an author.

An author has the right:

to publication, reproduction and distribution of his work by all legal means under his own name, a pseudonym or anonymously;

to the inviolability of his work;

to receive compensation for the use of his work by other people, except in cases provided for in law. The rates of compensation to authors are established by the legal authority of the U.S.S.R. and the Soviet republics.

Article 99. Co-authorship.

Copyright for works created by the combined efforts of two or more persons (collective work) belongs to the co-authors jointly whether the work is one unbroken whole or consists of parts, each of which has its own independent value. Each of the co-authors reserves his own copyright on the part of the collective work created by him and having its own independent value.

Article 100. Copyright for judicial persons. Copyright for works created while carrying out a duty assignment.

Judicial persons have copyright as established by the legal authority of the U.S.S.R. and the Soviet republics.

The author of a work created as part of a duty assignment in a scientific or other organization retains copyright to that work. Use

---

* Approved by the Supreme Soviet of the U.S.S.R. on December 8, 1961.

of such a work by the organization and compensation of the author are established by the legal authority of the U.S.S.R. and the Soviet republics.

Article 101. Use of an author's work by other people.

Use of an author's work by other people is only allowed on the basis of an agreement with the author or his descendants, except in cases provided in law.

Model agreements on the use of works (publication, presentation, film and other author's agreements) are established by the legal authority of the U.S.S.R. and Soviet republics.

Conditions in an author's agreement which put him in a less advantageous position than provided in law or model agreement are not legal and replaced by conditions provided in law or model agreement.

Article 102. Translation of a work into another language.

Any published work may be translated into another language without the consent but with notification of the author under condition that the integrity and thought of the work be retained. The right to compensation for use of the work in translation into another language remains with the author of the original as provided by the legal authority of the Soviet republics.

The translator may copyright his translation.

Article 103. Use of a work without the author's consent and without compensating the author.

Without the consent of the author and without compensating the author, but with mandatory indication of the name of the author whose work is being used and the source of the adaptation, one may:

1) use the published work of another to create a new artistic independent work, other than reworking narrative works into dramatic or scenarios or vice versa and reworking dramatic works into scenarios or vice versa;
2) reproduce in scientific and critical works, textbooks and political-educational publications, individual publications in science, literature and art and excerpts from them as provided by the legal authority of the Soviet republics;
3) use information in periodicals, films or on radio and television about published works in literature, science and art;
4) reproduce in newspapers, films, on radio and television publicly delivered speeches, reports and published works in literature, science or art;
5) reproduce by any means except mechanical contact copying, works of fine art located in places open to the public, except exhibitions and museums.

Article 104. Use of an author's work without his consent but with compensation.

Without the consent of the author but with an indication of his name and with compensation, one may:

1) present public performances of published works; however if the spectators do not pay, the author has the right to compensation only in cases prescribed by the legal authority of the Soviet republics;
2) record for public presentation or distribution works published on film, record, magnetic tape or another medium except productions in movies, on radio or television (point 4, article 103 of the present code);

3) use as a composer published literary works to create musical works with text;
4) use works of fine art and photographic works in industrial departments; in these cases the name of the author need not be indicated.

Article 105. Period of validity of copyright.

Copyright is retained by the author for life. The legal authority of the Soviet republics may establish shorter periods of copyright for individual types of works.

Copyright passes to the author's heirs in the order and within the limits fixed by the legal authority of the U.S.S.R. and the Soviet republics. If the period of the copyright has been shortened, it passes to the heirs for the unexpired time.

The legal authority of the Soviet republics establishes the limits of copyright for heirs, including compensation in relation to the sum involved, but never greater than 50 percent of the compensation which would have gone to the author himself.

Article 106. Purchase of copyright by the government.

Copyright to publication, public performance or any use of a work can be summarily purchased by the government from the author or his descendants as provided by the legal authority of the Soviet republics.

APPENDIX C

ALL-UNION MODEL PUBLISHING CONTRACT FOR LITERARY WORKS*

In carrying out the charge of February 16, 1967, from the Council of Ministers of the U.S.S.R., I order:

1. Affirmation and implementation from the 1st of June 1967 of agreements with the Ministry of Finance of the U.S.S.R., the State Committee of the Council of Ministers of the U.S.S.R. on labor and wage questions, and the Judicial Commission of the Council of Ministers of the U.S.S.R.:

    a) Model publishing agreement for literary and artistic works in accordance with appendix 1;

    b) Model publishing agreement for political, scientific, technical, scholarly and other literature (except literary and artistic) in accordance with appendix 2.

2. Establishment of the following order for implementation of the model agreements:

    a) Model agreements are to be used in negotiations after June 1, 1967;

    b) Negotiations between publishers and authors before June 1, 1967, are to use those rights and obligations which become effective after June 1, 1967, in setting the conditions of the agreements;

    c) Rights arising before June 1, 1967, but not declared valid at that moment by the legal authority are to conform to the regulations of the model publishing agreements.

3. All model publishing agreements for literary works are binding on all publishers regardless of their superior agency.

4. Central publishers and publishers of the committees on printing of the Soviet republics to strictly observe the requirements of the new model publishing agreements in concluding and implementing specific agreements on literary works.

5. Committee on printing of the Soviet republics to issue orders of observance after June 1, 1967, of the model agreements in the Soviet republics and in unavoidable cases to go into the established order with the responsible officials in the appropriate agency.

---

* Order of the Chairman of the Press Committee of the Council of Ministers of the U.S.S.R., No. 169, dated April 10, 1967.

MODEL PUBLISHING AGREEMENT FOR LITERARY AND ARTISTIC WORKS*

City_____19_____

    Publisher_____, called
hereafter "Publisher" in the person of director_____, acting
for the publisher, on the one side, and_____, hereafter
called "Author" on the other side, have concluded the present agreement
about the following:

    1. The Author will furnish or obligates himself to create and
furnish the Publisher for publication and republication his work
entitled_____(publication No.____), written in the
_____language, up to_____signatures in length (including
appendixes and illustrations), counting 40,000 characters to the
signature, or_____lines of verse, for a period of three years from
the day of acceptance of the manuscript by the Publisher or from the
day of signing the agreement, if it is concluded for a work in finished
form.

    For works consisting of two or more volumes, the period indicated
is counted from the day of acceptance of the manuscript of the last
volume by the Publisher except when each volume is published separately.

    Illustrative and other material (bibliographic, reference, and
indexes and commentaries) relevant to the manuscript can not exceed
_____% of the length of the work.

> Note: Counting the number of characters is done as for typograph-
> ical work in which spaces, half-titles, column headings
> and figures are not counted. Counting lines of verse is on
> the basis of the number of the author's lines, including
> headings.

    2. The work must meet the following conditions:

      a)_____.

          (Type of literature, genre)
      b) correspond to the prospectus (claim) accompanying the
         present agreement;
      c)_____.

    3. The manuscript of the work named in article 1, illustrative
material and other material must be furnished the Publisher by the
Author in printable form in two copies typed double-spaced on one side
of a standard sheet (30 typed lines with 57-58 characters to the line,
counting spaces between words) not later than"____" _____19_____.

    The Author has one additional month (beyond the agreed time) to
send the Publisher the manuscript for works of an agreed length of less
than 10 signatures and two additional months for works of an agreed
length of more than 10 signatures. The date of postmark on manuscripts
sent by mail is considered the date sent to the Publisher.

    Works created by two or more persons (collective works) are
signed by all co-authors and sent to the Publisher as a whole.

    If the manuscript is presented incomplete or in violation of
requirements for its external composition, the Publisher is within his
rights to return it to the Author with an indication of the reasons why
the manuscript was not accepted and a period of time for the Author to
correct the deficiencies of the manuscript. The Publisher can use this
right for a period of time equal to one day for each signature in the
actual manuscript, but not exceeding 10 days from the day of receipt.

---

*Order of the Chairman of the Committee on Printing of the Council of
Ministers of the U.S.S.R., No. 169, dated April 10, 1967.

At the end of this period, the manuscript is considered by the Author to have been presented in the proper form.

4. The Author obliges himself during the period of the agreement starting from the moment of signing that neither himself nor another person will publish his work or a part of it even under a different title, without prior written agreement of the Publisher. If this condition is violated, the Publisher can declare the agreement null.

Note. Until the Publisher has published the work, the Author is within his rights to publish it in newspapers, journals and "novel-newspapers".

5. The Publisher is obligated to pay the Author royalties for the work named in article 1 at current rates, separately for each type of material (original, compilation, commentary, illustrative, etc.) computed from the following rates for one signature or line of verse:

Royalties are paid:

a) with a publication run of not more than_____copies.
(In publishing literary and artistic works in greater runs, the Author is paid additional royalties in amounts fixed in the decrees for author's royalties);
b) for works for which a standard run is not established, irrespective of the run of the publication.

The order number of the publication is indicated in the agreement and fixed exactly by the Publisher in the final calculation of the given publication.

6. The royalties indicated in article 5 are to be paid to the Author at the following times:

a) upon concluding the agreement for a literary order, as an advance, in those cases and amounts set by the decrees for Author's royalties;
b) upon accepting the manuscript, 60% (deducting any advance paid) of the preliminary estimate of the length of the work;
c) the remaining sum in a final accounting, based on the actual length of the published work after signing the last sheet of the galley proof over to printing.

Author's royalties for runs in excess of the established standard are paid after publication.

Note. The Publisher has 14 days in which to pay each part of the royalties.

7. Royalties for reprinting works without revision while the agreement is still in force are paid at the following times:

a) 50% of the royalties not later than 7 days after receiving notification from the Author that he has no objection to the Publisher reprinting his work without revision or 7 days after the waiting period for receiving such notification (article 16);
b) 50% of the royalties after actual publication.

8. A manuscript is considered accepted by the Publisher if in the time periods indicated in notes 1 and 2 of the present article, he does not send the following:

a) justified written refusal to accept the manuscript because of unsuitability of the work itself;
b) written proposal to the Author that he must rework or correct his manuscript with exact specifications of what needs work or correction within the limits of the agreement.

When an agreement is concluded after acceptance of a manuscript, this fact is indicated in the text of the agreement.

Note 1. The periods for written notification prescribed in the present article are 30 days plus 4 days for each signature.

The time periods are figured from the day the Author submits the manuscript to the Publisher or from the day the Publisher receives the manuscript by mail. For calculating time periods for accepting works in verse, one signature equals 700 lines of verse.

Note 2. Submission of the manuscript for review by the responsible organization, when this is required by regulations, precedes the periods for notification of the Author as indicated in note 1 to article 8 while the manuscript is being reviewed plus two weeks.

9. The Author must be given sufficient time, agreed upon by both sides, to rework and correct his manuscript as provided in point (b) of article 8 and resubmit it to the Publisher. The corrected manuscript is considered accepted by the Publisher if in half the time provided in note 1 to article 8 he does not send the Author a written proposal for additional reworking or correcting of the manuscript or a written refusal to accept the manuscript. The manuscript can be refused if the Author did not rework or correct the manuscript as the Publisher proposed or did not carry out the instructions given by the Publisher.

10. The Publisher may nullify the agreement and recover from the Author royalties received (including any advance) on the following bases:

a) failure of the Author to submit the manuscript in time established in the agreement (including additional time) or in the time allowed for reworking it;
b) refusal of the Author to correct the manuscript as proposed, within the terms of the agreement;
c) completion of the work unscrupulously or not in accord with the conditions of the agreement (theme, special conditions, and length and genre, if changing the length and genre is not justified artistically); unscrupulousness is determined by a court;
d) violation of the Author of the obligation to personally create the work;
e) violation of the Author of the obligation set forth in article 4 of the agreement.

11. The Publisher has the right to decline a manuscript for unsuitability without sending it for review.

In declining a manuscript for unsuitability (point (a) of article 8), the Publisher has the right to nullify the agreement but without return of any advance by the Author.

12. The Publisher is obliged to publish a work not later than the following time periods: one year for a work of less than 10 signatures and two years for a work of more than 10 signatures, counting from the day of acceptance of the manuscript. For multicolored works 5 to 10 signatures long, the period for publishing can be extended to one and one-half years.

Subsequent editions are published in the same time periods.

13. If the Publisher does not publish an accepted work in the time periods indicated in article 12, he is obliged upon demand by the Author to pay him in full. The Author is also entitled to rescind the agreement and demand return of copies of his manuscript from the Publisher.

The Author does not have the right to rescind the agreement and demand return of his manuscript if the manuscript is not signed.

Note. If the Publisher proves that he could not publish the work because of circumstances depending on the Author, he is relieved of the obligation to pay the Author the part of the royalty indicated in point (c) of article 6 or point (b) of article 7 of the present agreement.

14. If the work accepted by the Publisher is not to be published because of state security, then the agreement is declared null. In this case the Author keeps his part of the royalties which he was entitled to have before the agreement was nullified.

15. The Publisher has the right to publish a work in any size run. Required, control and publicity copies of a work in not more than 150 copies are not counted in computing the Author's royalty.

Within the established time, each edition can be published in parts and at different times.

16. A Publisher is obliged to notify the Author of his decision to republish a work. Within two weeks of receiving notification of republication, the Author must notify the Publisher of his intention to modify the work. If no answer is received from the Author in this time, the Publisher has the right to republish the work without revision.

If the Publisher in republishing asks the Author to revise his work (except for statistical corrections and elimination of errors) or makes a similar proposition to the Author, the two parties make a new publishing agreement.

17. If the work accepted by the Publisher can not be published because of circumstances beyond the control of both parties, but it can be published with reworking and correction, the Author is obliged to rework and correct it. In this case a time for reworking and correcting is agreed upon in writing. If the Author refuses to rework or correct as proposed, the Publisher can nullify the agreement. The consequences of nullification are determined by the note to article 13 of the agreement.

The work is considered reworked and corrected if the Author receives no written notification from the Publisher within 20 days that additional work or new corrections are needed.

18. The Publisher reserves the right to refuse to republish a work. Written refusal of the Publisher to republish a work gives the Author the right to dispose of this work on his own and before the expiration of the agreement.

19. With the agreement of the Author, the Publisher can provide the work with illustrations, forewords, epilogues, commentaries and other explanatory materials.

20. On demand of the Publisher, the Author is obliged to furnish a certificate that the work written under the agreement is not planned work created in a scientific or higher educational institution while performing an assigned task, or a dissertation completed while interrupting production.

21. The Author is obliged on demand of the Publisher to read the galley of his work without special payment. In turn, the Publisher on demand of the Author is obliged to allow him to read the galley. The time for reading galleys is agreed upon between the Publisher and the Author within the limits provided by the flow charts for publishing books. The time required to send galleys is not counted. Delay of the galleys by the Author (longer than the set period) without overriding reasons as well as refusal of the Author to return galleys gives the

Publisher the right to print the work without the Author's corrections or delay its publication while the Author holds the galleys.

If the cost of correcting the galleys (except typographical errors and errors caused by unavoidable changes and inserts) exceeds 10 percent of the cost of type-setting, the Author pays for this excess up to 20% of the royalties.

Costs in printing the publication incurred by demand or fault of the Author can be recovered by the Publisher from the Author either by deducting from the amount paid the Author (point (c) of article 6) or by judicial ruling.

22. The Publisher is obliged to give the Author 10 copies of the first edition free and on demand up to 50 copies more at nominal cost. He is obliged to give the Author 2 free copies of all subsequent editions.

Note. Compliance with the demand of the Author is obligatory provided it was made before publication.

23. The Publisher has the right to transfer in full or in part the rights and obligations contained in the present agreement to another government or social organization.

24. Special conditions_____

25. Address of the Publisher_____

Address of the Author_____

The parties are obliged to inform each other of changes of address. Disputes over the present agreement are to be resolved by the prescribed legal code.

Director of publishing house

Author

APPENDIX D

HANDBOOK OF STANDARD PROVISIONS FOR THE PUBLISHING INDUSTRY

Table of Contents

I.   GENERAL REGULATIONS   Page

Committee on Printing of the Council of Ministers of the
    U.S.S.R.   4

Regulation for the order of coordinating publication of
    literature in the U.S.S.R.   9

Regulation for socialist state publishing   14

Creation and use of a fund for material encouragement and a fund
    for social and cultural enterprises and building in social-
    ist state publishing houses converted to the new system of
    planning and economic stimulation   30

Provisional model regulation for rewarding workers in publish-
    ing houses converting to the new system of planning and
    economic stimulation   36

Standards for determining the staff of editorial personnel of
    book and journal publishers   41

Attracting personnel in publishing houses to creative literary
    work   53

Basic units of measure for publishing production (system,
    determination, implementation). Departmental standard
    No. 14   54

Instruction for computing the length of literary production in
    printer's sheets   59

Instruction for computing the length of book, journal and
    artistic publications in publisher's sheets   64

Retail price list No. 116a for books, artwork, scores and
    covers   67

II.   PREPARATION OF MANUSCRIPTS FOR PUBLICATION

Model regulation for preparing manuscripts for publication   92

Technical requirements for preparing and marking up original
    texts for book and journal publications   110

Formats for books and journals (GOST 5773-68)   121

Formats for various types of publications   124

Formats for journals, serial publications and bulletins   128

Coefficients of capacity of sheets of composition in a
    60x90 1/16 format, composition format 6x9 1/4 sq.,
    10 point   129

Types of covers   131

Thickness of cardboard in mm. recommended for covers (depending on the number of the cover, the format and the thickness of the book)   132

III.   RELATIONSHIP OF PUBLISHERS TO AUTHORS AND ARTISTS

Copyright. Taken from the basic civil code of the U.S.S.R. and Soviet republics   134

All-Union model publishing agreements for literary productions   137

Author's royalties   150

Literary, Artistic and Musical Funds of the U.S.S.R.   176

IV.   RELATIONSHIP OF PUBLISHERS TO PUBLISHING ENTERPRISES

Supplying Paper and Binding Materials

Basic conditions for publishing enterprises to fill publishers' orders for producing books, journals and colored artwork   181

Author's and editor's corrections   208

Provisional model flow charts of book production   212

Basic conditions for centralized supplying of paper and cover materials to organizations and enterprises directly subordinate to the Committee on Printing of the Council of Ministers of the U.S.S.R.   231

Order for paying for paper and cover materials bought by publishing houses of the Main Publishing Administration (Glavpoligrafprom) for producing publications under the Committee on Printing of the Council of Ministers of the U.S.S.R.   251

Consolidated standards for using paper in the production of books, journals and artworks (for calculating and dividing paper funds among publishers)   253

Standards of paper use for technical production requirements   257

Standards of cardboard use for technical production requirements   282

Standards of commercial cloth use for technical production requirements   282

Paper and Cover Materials

Paper   285

Cover board (GOST 7950-56)   312

Cover cloths   316

Wholesale prices for products of the cellulose and paper industries   322

Wholesale prices for cover materials   326

Cover materials (cloth and paper base)   331

ILLUSTRATIVE MATERIAL ON STANDARD RETAIL PRICE SCHEDULES

PRICE LIST No. 116a

Retail Prices (Face Values) for Books, Pictorial Works,
Musical Notes and Covers*

I. Face Value of Books, Pamphlets and Albums (without Covers)

Kinds of Literature	Face Value of a Printer's Sheet in Kopecks	
	No. 1 Paper	No. 2 and 3 Paper

1. Political, social-economic and legal literature

1. Collected works and separate basic works of Marxism-Leninism, Communist Party materials, and works of Party and government leaders of the U.S.S.R.	2,4	2,1
2. Agitator and popular literature	2,1	1,8
3. Collected works on social and political science	4,3	4,0
4. Biographies of the founders of Marxism-Leninism; materials of foreign Communist Parties and works of international Communist and labor leaders; popular political and legal works; trade-union, Komsomol and Pioneer publications; popular reference works and documentary literature	2,6	2,3
5. Popular literature in the humanities, journalism and memoirs	3,2	2,9
6. Reference material and collections of archival materials and documents for specialists; practical legal reference materials	3,8	3,5
7. Limited-edition, special-purpose, practical legal materials	5,3	5,0

*Established by Order No. 155, dated May 27, 1965, of the Press
Committee of the Council of Ministers of the U.S.S.R.

8. Scientific and scho-
    larly works of
    institutions of research
    and higher education;
    monographs on philosophy,
    scientific socialism,
    dialectical and historical
    materialism, economics,   6,3   6,0
    history, history of the
    C.P.S.U., law, psychology,
    linguistics and other
    humanities, international
    problems and trade-union
    movements

> Note: For monographs published in many copies for a large
>   group of readers, the face value is the same as for
>   popular science literature.

PRINTING EQUIPMENT IMPORTS OF THE U.S.S.R.
(1,000 rubles)

Country	1960	1961	1968	1969
Soviet Bloc	13,401	15,085		
Czechoslovakia	--	--	2,492	2,300
East Germany	11,333	11,850	14,104	13,826
Hungary	1,403	2,085	481	541
Rumania	665	1,150	--	--
Other Countries	857	935		
Austria	673	668	--	--
Finland	184	267	--	--
France	--	--	457	1,928
Great Britain	--	--	1,914	4,128
Japan	--	--	138	380
Switzerland	--	--	2,309	1,366
West Germany	--	--	3,126	2,867
Denmark	--	--	87	224
Italy	--	--	1,010	525
West Berlin	--	--	60	100
Unspecified	27	107	--	--
Total	14,285	16,127	26,178	28,185

Source: Vneshniaia Torgovlia Soiuza SSR, 1969, Tables XVIII & XIX, page 98.

GENERAL PUBLISHING STATISTICS, 1969

Appendix Table 1

TYPES OF SOVIET PUBLICATIONS

Type	Number of Titles, 1969	Number of Titles, 1968	Press Run, 1969 (in thousands)	Press Run, 1968 (in thousands)
Non-Periodicals				
Books & brochures	74,587	75,699	1,315,721	1,334,005
Posters, portraits, etc.	14,634	13,621	2,309,426	2,168,255
Calendars	11	16	38,510	39,200
Music	1,832	1,615	20,489	17,994
Dissertations (author reference)	19,817	22,802	3,963	4,560
Maps	(not given)	361	(not given)	19,893
Periodicals & Continuing Publications				
Magazines	1,185	1,135	1,867,616	1,692,536
Bloknoty Agitatora	65	76	31,728	45,410
Collections (works, trudy, etc.)	2,003	1,846	70,776	59,123
Bulletins	2,300	2,052	599,721	565,252
Newspapers	7,514	7,307	29,426,738	27,810,438
Kolkhoz newspapers	1,510	1,447	19,910	18,128

Source: Table 1, Pechat'S.S.S.R., 1969

Appendix Table 2

NUMBER OF NEW TITLES (BOOKS AND PAMPHLETS) PUBLISHED,
BY PUBLISHING CENTER, 1969

Rank by no. of titles	City	No. of titles	Total Press Run
1	Moscow[1]	34,082	882,908,000
2	Kiev[1]	4,843	110,895,000
3	Leningrad[1]	3,699	51,858,000
4	Tbilisi	2,080	16,887,000
5	Riga	1,990	14,943,000
6	Minsk[1]	1,850	23,929,000
7	Alma-Ata[1]	1,823	22,861,000
8	Vilnius	1,710	10,311,000
9	Tashkent[1]	1,680	32,626,000
10	Tallin	1,528	11,179,000
11	Kishliev	1,307	10,150,000
12	Yerevan	1,090	10,151,000
13	Baku	985	9,872,000
14	Khar'kov[1]	898	2,512,000
15	Frunzo	829	5,748,000
16	Novosibirsk[1]	690	4,358,000
17	Dushanbe	640	5,281,000
18	Svordlovsk[1]	549	3,634,000
19	Odessa[1]	484	1,959,000
20	Kazan'[2]	467	5,678,000
	Total:	63,224	1,237,740,000
	All other:	11,373	77,981,000
	Grand total:	74,597	1,315,721,000

[1]Figures include titles published in surrounding oblast.

[2]Figure includes titles published in surrounding autonomous republic.

Other figures indicate titles published in city only.

Source: Table 42, Pechat'S.S.S.R., 1969

57

Appendix Table 3

NUMBER OF NEW TITLES (BOOKS AND PAMPHLETS) PUBLISHED, BY REPUBLIC, 1969

Rank	Republic	No. Titles	Leading Cities	
1	R.S.F.S.R.	47,133	Moscow	33,497
			Leningrad	3,682
2	Ukraine	8,015	Kiev[1]	4,843
			Khar'kov[1]	898
3	Georgia	2,302	Tbilisi	2,080
4	Lithuania	2,177	Vilnius	1,710
5	Latvia	2,042	Riga	1,990
6	Byelorussia	2,008	Minsk[1]	1,850
7	Kazakhstan	1,986	Alma-Ata[1]	1,823
8	Uzbekistan	1,894	Tashkent[1]	1,680
9	Estonia	1,703	Tallin	1,528
10	Moldavia	1,330	Kishinev	1,307
11	Armenia	1,093	Yerevan	1,090
12	Azerbaidjan	1,075	Baku	985
13	Kirgizstan	838	Frunze	829
14	Tadzhikstan	655	Dushanbe	640
15	Turkmenistan	336	Ashkhabad	331

[1]Includes titles published in surrounding oblast.

Source: Table 41, Pechat'S.S.S.R., 1969

Appendix Table 4

NUMBER OF NEW TITLES (BOOKS AND PAMPHLETS) PUBLISHED,
BY LANGUAGE

Language	No. Titles 1969	No. Titles 1968
Russian	57,048	57,498
Ukrainian	3,061	2,950
Georgian	1,684	1,568
Lithuanian	1,476	1,505
Estonian	1,293	1,316
Latvian	1,088	1,013
Uzbek	887	870
Armenian	867	907
Azeri	660	863
Kazakh	637	599
Moldavian	514	557
Byelorussian	425	453
Kirgiz	410	404
Tadzhik	343	350
Tatar	229	235
Turkmen	207	274
Karakalpak	150	124
Bashkir	97	104
Chuvash	91	87
Uigur	81	55
. . . .	. .	. .
Yiddish	8	2

Foreign Language	No. Titles 1969	No. Titles 1968
English	952	1,389
French	382	425
German	358	364
Spanish	145	187
All Indian Languages (Hindi, Bengali, etc.)	80	76
Hungarian	57	71
Polish	45	51
. . . .	. .	. .
Chinese	8	5
. . . .	. .	. .
Romanian	3	11

Languages of the U.S.S.R., total:	72,137	72,651
Foreign Languages, total:	2,450	3,048
Grand total:	74,587	75,699

Source: Table 6, Pechat' S.S.S.R., 1969

Book Publishing
IN THE
U·S·S·R

REPORT OF THE DELEGATION
OF U.S. BOOK PUBLISHERS
VISITING THE U.S.S.R.

August 20-September 17
1962

Curtis G. Benjamin   *Storer B. Lunt*

Kurt Enoch   *M. R. Robinson*

Robert W. Frase   *W. B. Wiley*

The report which follows was prepared by the group of book publishers which visited the U.S.S.R. under the official U.S. - U.S.S.R. Exchanges Agreement for 1962-63 signed in Washington on March 8, 1962. A similar group of Soviet specialists in book publishing is scheduled to come to the United States on a reciprocal visit.

The Department of State welcomes the preparation of reports such as this one by the U.S. groups which go to the Soviet Union under the exchanges program. Such reports contribute to the purposes of the program by making available to broad business and professional circles as well as to the general public the information and impressions gained by groups of specialists which are necessarily limited in size. The Department is also grateful to the companies and individual businessmen assuming the considerable expenses involved in making such trips to the Soviet Union, as well as to the trade associations which shoulder the responsibility of the programs for the return visits to the United States of exchange groups. The exchange program could not operate successfully without this generous support in time and money from business and other private sources.

Ralph A. Jones
Deputy Director
Soviet and Eastern European Exchanges Staff
U. S. Department of State
Washington 25, D. C.

Members of the delegation of U.S. book publishers to the U.S.S.R.
August - September 1962

Curtis G. Benjamin
Chairman of Board
McGraw-Hill Book Company
330 West 42nd Street
New York 36, New York
Chairman, Joint Committee on Copyright of the
    American Book Publishers Council (ABPC) and the
    American Textbook Publishers Institute (ATPI)

Kurt Enoch
President
New American Library
501 Madison Avenue
New York 22, New York
Member of Board of Directors, ABPC

Storer B. Lunt
Chairman of Board
W. W. Norton and Company, Inc.
55 Fifth Avenue
New York 3, New York
Chairman of the Committee on Reading Development, ABPC
Member, Executive Committee, International Publishers Association

M. R. Robinson
President
Scholastic Book Services
50 West 44th Street
New York 36, New York
President, American Textbook Publishers Institute

W. B. Wiley
President
John Wiley and Sons, Inc.
440 Park Avenue South
New York 16, New York
Chairman, Joint Committee on International Trade of
    the ABPC and the ATPI

Robert W. Frase
Director, Joint Washington Office of the ABPC and the ATPI
1820 Jefferson Place, N.W.
Washington 6, D. C.

I. INTRODUCTION

The U.S.A.-U.S.S.R. Cultural Exchanges Agreement for
1962-1963 was signed on March 8, 1962. In accordance with the
Agreement, the objective of the American book publishers visiting the U.S.S.R. was to be two fold:

1. "To make a study of the methods of book selection,
   the printing of books and their distribution;"

2. "To encourage the exchange of books, magazines,
   newspapers and other publications devoted to
   scientific, technical, cultural and general
   educational subjects both through commercial
   channels and between the libraries, universities
   and other organizations of each country."

Also related to the book industry was a provision of the Agreement providing for an exhibit of technical books from each country in three to four cities of the other country. Finally, a
comparable group of U.S.S.R. publishers is scheduled to visit
the U.S.A. in 1963.

On March 20th the representatives of the American Book
Publishers Council and the American Textbook Publishers Institute
met in Washington to formalize the details of the proposed
exchange. Our preliminary request for six publishers and for a
full month's survey - as opposed to five publishers for three
weeks - was presented.

Subsequently the six American delegates were named by the
presidents of both the Council and the Institute. Messrs. W. B.
Wiley and M. R. Robinson were to represent the Institute.
Messrs. K. Enoch and S. B. Lunt were to represent the Council.
Messrs. C. G. Benjamin and R. W. Frase were joint appointees of
both organizations. Mr. Benjamin was designated chairman, with
Mr. Frase serving as secretary of the delegation.

In the official acceptance of our proposals by the
U.S.S.R. dated July 12th our suggestions as to the number of
delegates and the four week duration of the visit to the U.S.S.R.

were accepted. We were requested to appear in Moscow on August 20th. Prior to leaving the U.S.A., there were consultations in Washington with those officially concerned and we also met with officials in the Embassy of the U.S.S.R.

Before proceeding to Moscow we assembled as a delegation in London and there we were guests at a luncheon given by the British Publishers Association. Two of the British publishers present had also been to the U.S.S.R. on a publishing mission. The London publishers were generous with helpful information, and it became clear that along with a common language, we both share common problems and that we will do well to work closely together and keep each other informed of further developments. It should here be pointed out that English is the principal world language used in the U.S.S.R., being increasingly taught in the schools and widely known. On the return trip via London, two of the delegation met again with the British publishers and reported informally on our visit.

We made it our business to see as much of as many of the leading people in the U.S.S.R. book industry - officials, publishers, printers, book distributors, authors, librarians, managers of bookstores of various types - and to explore and study as many areas of the industry as could be managed. This offered many opportunities to register and underline the importance of the Universal Copyright Convention, and its long-term real advantages to all countries, including the U.S.S.R., and also to explore ways and means whereby U.S. publications could be made more available to the people of the U.S.S.R.

Moscow made the major claim on our time both at the outset and at the termination of our visit, but distinct and important findings came from our visits of several days each to Leningrad, Kiev, Sochi and Alma Ata along with neighboring villages and one visit to a collective farm. At our first meeting with the Soviet State Committee for the Coordination of Scientific Research, one of our hosts, the U.S.S.R. officials accommodated our every request both on our itinerary and on our appointments in each locality to be visited. Official cars were always available to us, and we were met and seen off by local government officials and publishing representatives wherever we went. Further, arrangements for conferences - some 50 altogether - were meticulously planned; and directors with their management subordinates were prepared to talk freely and information was fully given. Our questions were countered with responsive and factual answers in practically every instance. Our final official meeting in Moscow was with Mrs. Furtseva, the U.S.S.R. Minister of Culture, with whom the discussions were very frank, timely and pointed.

We were fortunate in being accompanied throughout our visit by two English-speaking representatives of the U.S.S.R. publishing industry: Mr. N. Sabetski, a skilled and experienced author, editor and deputy director of the U.S.S.R. Publishing House of Foreign Literature, and his younger colleague, Mr. O. Sergeyev, who served as interpreter. The delegation was particularly fortunate in having during our entire stay the knowledgeable skills and expert guidance of Mr. Herbert S. Okun, then Second Secretary of the U.S. Embassy in Moscow. To these three gentlemen go our acknowledgment and our thanks.

It is usual in a report such as this to state that within so limited a time a complete picture could not be obtained. This is so. A complete picture could not be secured; but we feel that it may be fairly stated that once we understood the pattern of the organization of the Soviet book industry, we developed a very fair grasp of the methods of operating it. In this report we have cited exact statistics from documentary sources wherever possible. When such sources were not available we have given as approximations figures from our notes which had been provided to us orally in our conferences with Soviet bookmen. This report has been authored by each one of us and the facts and opinions here expressed are shared by the entire delegation.

II. ORGANIZATION OF BOOK PUBLISHING

"The organization of the book publishing industry of the U.S.S.R. is a very complicated matter."

This was the opening statement by the chairman of our host committee in our first working conference in Moscow. We knew it to be true because we had tried to prepare ourselves by advance readings of the excellent book PUBLISHING IN THE U.S.S.R. by Boris I. Gorokhoff (Indiana University, 1959). But even with Mr. Gorokhoff's systematic and detailed guide in hand, we often had reason to recall this opening statement. For as we went along, we found it difficult to fit bits and pieces of information into the complicated over-all organizational structure of a state-owned and state-controlled book publishing system.

There are at present a total of 320 publishing houses in the U.S.S.R. Most of them are under the direct control of governmental ministries on one of three levels: the national U.S.S.R. (All-Union) level, the Republic level, or the province (oblast) level. The remaining houses are under the control of professional, educational, labor and party organizations such as academies of sciences, unions of writers and universities. These organizations are in turn responsible to ministries or sub-agencies of government.

A national U.S.S.R. book publishing house usually serves a specialized interest of the entire Soviet Union and is known as a State or "central" house. A Union Republic house may serve either the general or a specialized interest of one of the fifteen Republics making up the U.S.S.R. and is known as a "Republic" house. A provincial house serves the still narrower interests of a still smaller national minority or territorial unit, and as it usually issues publications of all kinds, it is often called a "universal" house.

A majority of these 320 publishing houses are small in size. This accounts for the fact that a few of the larger

national houses (18 or 20) publish about 65% of all the books
produced in the U.S.S.R. annually. Further, almost all of the
large central houses are located in Moscow, and it is estimated
that 70% of Soviet book publishing is administered from that
city.

There is no over-all administrative agency for all the
government-owned central houses. Rather all such houses are
responsible, either individually or in organized groups, to
ministers or other officials of the Council of Ministers (Sovet
Ministrov).

Although the Republic houses are under the administration
of the Republic governments, they usually are subordinate to
central agencies in matters of planning and policy. And the
provincial houses usually are subordinate to Republic agencies
in the same manner.

Of the several large organizational complexes for Soviet
book publishing, the one under the U.S.S.R. Ministry of Culture
is the largest and probably the most important. Here the
Ministry's Publishing House Branch (commonly called Glavizdat)
is organized for:

1. Direct control of thirteen large "central"
    publishing houses.

2. Allocation of paper and printing facilities
    to these houses.

3. Direct control of the Ministry's network of
    book trade agencies commonly called Knigotorg.
    (See Chapter IV).

This administrative agency also has indirect planning and policy
control over 111 smaller houses, most of which are organized
either directly or indirectly under the ministries of culture of
the union republics.

A listing of the 15 central houses under the U.S.S.R.
Ministry of Culture, together with a brief description and a
record of the 1961 output of each, is given in Table 1.

The Ministry of Culture also has jurisdiction over the

publications of the All-Union Book Chamber, located in the Lenin
State Library (see Chapter V), and over the large and important
publishing program of the U.S.S.R. Union of Writers (see Chapter
VIII).

Another large and important All-Union book publishing
complex is the Association of Scientific and Technical Publishing Houses (ONTIZ), which was organized in 1958 and is now under
the State Committee for the Coordination of Scientific Research.
(This committee jointly with Glavizdat was responsible for planning our itinerary and conferences in the U.S.S.R.) Five large
houses under this administration specialize in books on petro-
leum, mechanical engineering, metallurgy, mining, and fish and
other food products. Together they publish about 3100 new and
reissued books per year. (See Chapter IX).

In all the U.S.S.R. there are in addition to the ONTIZ
group 32 other houses producing specialized technical and industrial books. Each of these is in an industrial ministry or a
subordinate industrial or trade organization.

A third large publishing complex is the Publishing House
of the U.S.S.R. Academy of Sciences and the network of the
houses of the Republic academies. The central Academy is directly responsible to the U.S.S.R. Council of Ministers. The
U.S.S.R. Academy published 804 new and reissued book titles in
1961 and also issues 76 magazines and abstract journals. It is
administratively responsible for the Publishing House of
Oriental Literature, also located in Moscow, which produced 177
Russian-language books on Asiatic countries in 1961.

The publishing houses of the Republic academies of
science published 1012 titles in 1961, many of which were in the
minority languages of their respective areas.

Often there is more than one house in a specialized area,
but in each case there is a difference in type of book published.
For example: In addition to the large Children's Publishing
House (Detgiz) under the Ministry of Education of the Russian
Republic, there is another small publishing house for children's

literature under the U.S.S.R. Ministry of Culture,"Children's World."

Medical books are published by the State Medical Publishing House (Medgiz) under the administration of the U.S.S.R. Ministry of Public Health, which also publishes for the U.S.S.R. Academy of Medical Science and the RSFSR Ministry of Public Health as well. In addition to a large annual list of professional books, this house produces textbooks for secondary and higher medical schools, the U.S.S.R.'s "Large Medical Encyclopedia," and popular medical literature for mass distribution.

Encyclopedia publishing apparently is especially important in the U.S.S.R., for the State Scientific Publishing House "Great Soviet Encyclopedia" reports directly to the U.S.S.R. Council of Ministers. (See Chapter XIII).

Textbook publishing is organized on two levels. The U.S.S.R. Ministry of Higher Education is responsible for the planning and production of university and "institute" (college level) texts and for middle-level texts for "tekhnikum" (technical institute), home-study and evening courses. Each Union-Republic Ministry of Education is responsible for planning and producing texts for its own secondary and elementary schools. (See Chapter X).

Of specialized houses of the smaller "central" type and of the Republic or provincial type, there seemed to be no end. Accordingly no attempt will be made here to fit even a sampling of them into any organizational pattern. But the reader may be interested in brief descriptions of the organization of publishing in the two Union Republics visited by our delegation, the Ukraine and Kazakhstan.

There are 37 publishing houses in the Ukraine, of which 17 are Union-Republic houses under Republic administration and 20 are branches of central houses in Moscow. The Republic houses are organized under an administrative Glavizdat in the Ukrainian Ministry of Culture. This Glavizdat is also responsible for the administration of an autonomous Ukrainian

Knigotorg, which serves in a dual capacity as distributor of the books published by the Ukrainian houses and as the Republic branch of the All-Union Knigotorg in Moscow. It also allocates paper and printing facilities to the Republic printing houses.

All the Ukrainian houses together publish between 8,000 and 9,000 titles or editions annually. The primary purpose of the Republic houses is to serve the minority-language needs of the Republic. Accordingly, 70% of their output (in number of copies) is in the Ukrainian language and the remainder in Russian and the other minority languages of the Republic. About 120,000,000 copies are produced annually by all the Ukrainian houses.

In Kazakhstan, which is a smaller and more remote Republic in Central Asia (population 10 million), all book publishing and distribution activity is again organized under a Glavizdat in the Ministry of Culture of the Republic. There are five specialized publishing houses in this group, mostly producing books in the Kazakh language, but with some in Russian and minor languages:

1. House of Literature for Mass Distribution (Political and practical arts and popular science).
2. Belles-lettres House.
3. Textbook House (Texts at all levels and professional books in pedagogy).
4. Agricultural House.
5. Academy of Science House.

Here the local Glavizdat has direct administration of three large printing plants as well as the usual control of the Republic Knigotorg. In addition to books, it controls the publication of 19 magazines. In 1961 a total of 1,516 titles or editions of books and pamphlets were published in 16,000,000 copies. The Kazakh officials can, and do, point with great pride to this record of book production in a provincial area which was almost completely illiterate 40 years ago, and in which only 14 books were published in 20,000 copies in 1913.

Table 1

Publishing Houses in the
U.S.S.R. Ministry of Culture
1961 Production

Publishing House	Titles Published	Copies Produced
Geografgiz (Geography)	63	2,093,000
Gozlitizdat (Belles-lettres)	375	42,807,000
Gozpolitizdat (Political)	411	68,755,000
Gosiurizdat (Law)	209	7,187,000
Detski Mir (Children)	116	11,889,000
Foreign Literature (I.L.)	359	6,891,000
Dictionary (G.I.S.)	46	1,669,000
Izogiz (Pictorial Art)	8	215,000
Iskusstvo ("Art")	255	6,117,000
Muzgiz (Music)	97	1,464,000
Sotsekgiz	128	2,718,000
Physical Culture and Sport	98	3,073,000
Fizmatgiz (Physics & Mathematics)	191	6,380,000

(The following two are in the Ministry
but not under Glavizdat)

Book Chamber (Bibliographic)	32	283,000
Soviet Russia	323	14,430,000

III. OPERATION OF A PUBLISHING HOUSE

A Soviet publishing house usually is headed by a Director who has both editorial and operating responsibility for his organization. Each house has an Editorial Council which acts as an advisory board to the director in matters of planning and policy. Membership in the Council of each house is drawn from its officers, from the ministry or other official organization to which it reports, and from professionals and specialists in the field of its publications.

Usually there are two branches in each house, the Editorial Branch and the Production Branch. The former is headed by an Editor-in-Chief, who serves also as the first Assistant Director. The larger houses have several editorial sections, each under the direction of a Chief Editor. The Production Branch is on the same administrative level as the Editorial Branch, and its head serves as the second Assistant Director. This Branch usually is organized on a pattern that is very familiar to U.S. publishers - it has sections for planning and scheduling, technical editing, proofreading, graphics, quality control and estimating.

For general management, the accounting and service functions, also organized on familiar patterns, report to the Director. The Personnel Section is responsible for record keeping and for training and up-grading the workers' performance. This section also has a large part in the work of an Attestation Commission, an important body in each house. This Commission "periodically undertakes the evaluation of the scholarly, business, political and social aspects of the work of each employee," but hiring and firing remain the responsibility of the director through his line organization. The workers' unions seem to have a large hand in the discipline of delinquent and incompetent workers.

Every publishing house operates under an annual "thematic plan" which is prepared and officially approved in the late sum-

mer or early fall for the control of its activities in the following year. This "thematic plan" is a complete publishing program and an operating and production budget rolled into one.
In September 1962 we saw printed "thematic plans" of several
houses for 1963. They had the appearance of advance catalogs,
giving detailed information on all books scheduled for publication during the year - such specifics as authorship, title, size,
price, number of copies to be printed and prospective reader
interest.

The "thematic plan" serves as the basis on which working
capital, paper, and manufacturing facilities are allocated to
the house. It also serves as the standard of performance expected of workers and management, and hence as the base for
incentives and bonus payments, of which more will be said later.
To provide for unforeseen publishing opportunities that might
arise from new developments during the year, an uncommitted quota
of production capacity is provided in each plan. Further, although the plans seem to be viewed quite rigidly by the official
control agencies, they are subject to review and necessary adjust-
ment quarterly. We did not succeed in getting even a general
idea of how fully the advance plans were met by actual annual
performance in the average house.

Theoretically, wages, manufacturing costs and prices are
officially regulated so as to allow each publishing house to make
a modest profit on its annual operation under the approved "thematic plan." It is recognized, however, that in practice this is
not always possible or even desirable. The smaller houses, especially those serving minority-language or specialized scientific and cultural interests, are expected to operate at a loss.
The larger houses are expected to make up this loss by profit
returns to the state treasury. The over-all national policy and
objective is to produce all books considered necessary by the
Party and the government at the lowest possible prices for every
type of reader.

Paper, printing and binding facilities are provided each
house at official costs and rates that are standard throughout

the U.S.S.R. (A few of the larger central publishing houses own and control their own printing plants, but all other houses contract for their production to an assigned local plant or plants under the control of the regional economic council.) Wages and salaries also are standardized by official regulations, but in certain areas higher than standard rates have to paid to attract skilled workers. Royalties to authors also are paid on standard scales set by laws and regulations. (See Chapter XV).

Book prices also are set, under an official schedule of rates that applies throughout the U.S.S.R. (See Chapter V). In theory, pricing is regulated so that the cost of each book plus royalty and profit will equal 75% of the list price. Thus the publisher in effect sells his book to the state distributing agencies at a 25% discount; and his success in getting manufacturing and other costs, including royalty, under 75% of the list price, determines whether he has an operating profit or loss on each title.

The Soviet system of incentives for efficient and profitable operation of a publishing house is too complicated for anything other than a sketchy description here. It is, of course, tied directly to the annual "thematic plan." If a house succeeds in meeting its base plan for the year, a share of its profit, sometimes as much as 15%, goes into a "house" fund which is controlled by the director and a committee of the trade union of the workers. This fund is used for bonuses on wages and salaries of workers and management, for improved living conditions for the workers, for better social and recreational facilities, for paying vacations expenses, and for modernization of plant and equipment. If a house fails to meet its annual plan, this special fund is reduced in accordance with the degree of failure. But the worst that can happen to the workers is the complete elimination of the special fund; for them there is no negative penalty other than the failure to receive plus benefits. For the management, there may be more serious consequences. The enterprise first goes into debt to the industrial bank to the extent of the losses. If losses continue the management will eventually be changed. However, if investigation shows that the management was not to blame, the plan will be adjusted downward.

In publishing practice, the "thematic plan" of each house is supposed to produce a well-rounded program of the most interesting and useful new books needed in its area. The ultimate responsibility for the selection of titles, for filling gaps and avoiding needless duplication, rests with the director - working with the assistance and guidance of his Editorial Council, of course. In general the publishing program is developed largely from assigned and commissioned manuscripts and the publishing houses are less dependent on unsolicited submission of manuscripts than is the average U.S. house.

The director is responsible for negotiating and signing contracts with authors, but there is relatively little negotiating to be done since the general form of the contract is fixed by law and royalties are set by standard rates that permit only some variation for "quality". So on the whole there is not much variation or flexibility in the arrangement of a publishing contract.

The process of manuscript criticism and perfection is much the same there as in the United States, and so are the production processes, except that galley proofs are required only for the exceptionally difficult book. More of the responsibility for the finished form of the work is placed on the publishing house editor and less on the author than in the United States. This is reflected in the fact that the names of the responsible publishing house editors appear in the back of the books themselves. Authority and responsibility for making approved and acceptable printings are carefully regulated through control and signal copies, and every printed book contains a detailed record of editorial, quality and quantity printed. The following is an example of the information given for the 1961 edition of the statistical yearbook on publishing, Pechat SSSR:

Editor: V. A. Samuilov
Technical editor: N. I. Avrustis
Address of editorial office: B. Kommunisticheskaya
                                Street No. 15, Moscow
Telephone: Zh 2-19-41

—————

Manuscript submitted to printer: March 22, 1962
Approval for publication: April 19, 1962
Printer's sheets: 15.41
Publisher's sheets: 12:15
A-03268
Page size for printing: 70 x 108 1/16 centimeters
Printing: 2370 copies
Order No. 563
Publishing House of the All-Union Book Chamber,
Bryusovsky Perelok No. 8/10, Moscow K-9.

—————

Printing Plant of the All-Union Book Chamber,
Chaikovsky Street No. 20, Moscow G-9.

The question of censorship was never discussed to our satisfaction with anyone in the U.S.S.R. Everywhere we were told that there was no actual censorship of books, only "house" control over what was or was not suitable for publication in terms of a house's "charter" and of "state security". Yet most books printed for sale in the U.S.S.R. contain a code number that can be identified as censorship approval prior to publication. And Gorokhoff (p. 52) says that there probably is a censor on the staff of every publishing house, with a corps of assistants known as "political editors". The censor is subordinate to the director, but he and his assistants work under instructions from the central censorship agency, Glavlit. Anyone with a special interest in this subject will want to read Chapter VI of Mr. Gorokhoff's PUBLISHING IN THE U.S.S.R..

In contrast to his counterparts in other countries, the director of a Soviet publishing house has no headaches over a book once it has been printed, for he is always (or nearly always) assured of an immediate and full sale of each edition. This utopian aspect of his operation arises from centralized agencies of distribution to the domestic and foreign markets which assume full responsibility for sales and possible overstocks. (See Chapter IV).

Even though the distributing agencies are responsible for sales, the publishing houses are responsible for advertising and promotion. Almost no advertising in terms of American or European practice is done; almost all promotion of a new book is through simple listings, announcements and reviews. Newspapers, magazines and local radio and TV stations are widely used for announcements of a "it's ready - come and get it" nature. And much promotion of the same nature is done locally by bookstores. Also, author appearances in bookstores, with personal readings and autographing, are widely employed to sell popular poetry, fiction and music.

It was not surprising to hear in the distributing agencies some expressions of dissatisfaction with the present practice in promoting new books. Several officials expressed the opinion that the publishing houses were not meeting their responsibility adequately or effectively. Some of them expressed keen interest in our methods of space and direct-mail advertising and suggested that they might have to come to similar methods to accomplish really effective promotion in the U.S.S.R.

IV. BOOK DISTRIBUTION

As in the case of all publishing activities, book distribution is considered an instrument serving the cultural, educational and political aims of the State, and is controlled from
top to bottom by the State with hardly any consideration of
profit.

There are several distribution networks:

A. The All-Union Book Trade Association (Soiuzkniga),
briefly called the Knigotorg system, controlled by the Ministry
of Culture.

B. The cooperative network used to supply books to the
rural areas.

C. Soiuzpechat' mainly concerned with the distribution
of newspapers and magazines but to a small extent also with
books. An agency of the U.S.S.R. Ministry of Communications.

D. A number of special networks, such as the bookstores
of the U.S.S.R. Academy of Sciences, of the U.S.S.R. Union of
Writers, of the military book trade agency, of the railroad
book trade system and others.

The total number of retail book outlets in these networks seems to be close to 50,000.

Knigotorg

By far the most important network is the Knigotorg
system which accounts for approximately 80% of all book supply
and had in 1961 a sales volume of about 300,000,000 rubles.
(Total retail sales volume in 1961 for all printed publications
- newspapers and magazines as well as books and pamphlets -
was 840,000,000 rubles). The head office of Knigotorg is
located in Moscow. It has agencies in all Republics and in
some provinces which are subordinate to the local governments
but under the general direction of the central organization in
Moscow. It includes book stores and other retail outlets which
are not autonomous organizations but an integral part of Knigotorg. In other words, the Knigotorg system extends from the

receipt of books from publishers down to retail bookstore sales to consumers.

Through its system Knigotorg supplies not only Russian language books published in the Moscow area but also books published in other languages in the several Republics throughout the U.S.S.R. In addition, it is the main supplier of the book trade in the U.S.S.R. with foreign language books published by the Publishing House for Foreign Languages or imported by the import and export organization (Mezhdunarodnaia Kniga). Finally, it supplies books to so-called "book collectors" - organizations specialized in the supply of libraries - and to the cooperative stores as well as to the minor book distribution networks. A total of 10,500 book shops and 27,000 kiosks selling books only - exclusive of general shops which sell other merchandise as well - are directly or indirectly supplied through the Knigotorg network.

The Cooperative Stores

The cooperative network sells books in small towns and villages through bookstores, book kiosks and stores selling other merchandise in rural areas. It obtains its supply from the nearest local Knigotorg agency, usually on the provincial level. The Knigotorgs of the provinces supply the district cooperative bookstores which in turn supply the other stores in the area. The cooperative network in 1958 sold books in 3,406 bookstores, 20,000 village stores, 3,000 cultural stores and 2,000 district stores. Book sales volume in 1956 was 43 million rubles. We did not obtain later statistics, but it might be of interest that in Pereyaslav-Khmel'nitsky, a town with a population of 18,000 approximately 80 miles East of Kiev, the cooperative system operated one bookstore and three kiosks (handling books only). This bookstore alone had a sale of 28,000 rubles in 1961 and 25,600 rubles from January to August 1962. It had a stock of 3,000 titles including translations into the Ukranian language of such English and American authors as Mansfield, Graham Green, Stephen Crane, Fenimore Cooper, Jack London,

Galsworthy, O. Henry and Dreiser. The total number of stores
and kiosks in the cooperative system in that region was 60,
located in 60 villages, with a total population for the region
of 71,000. In the Republic of Kazakhstan, we were informed that
in 1961 the cooperative system supplied 353 outlets with books
having a total sales volume of 6,500,000 rubles to 7,300,000
rubles per year. By comparison there were under Knigotorg
directly eight bookstores and 21 book kiosks in the capital
city of Alma Ata, and a total of 202 bookstores in all the
Republic, with a total 1961 sale of 15,000,000 rubles.

Soiuzpechat'

This organization, mainly concerned with the distribution
of newspapers and magazines, is set up similar to the Knigotorg
system. It has a central office in Moscow, a branch in Leningrad and local offices in the Republics and provinces. It has
about 60,000 distribution points, including 10,000 kiosks selling books. It handles approximately 4,000 books and pamphlet
titles. A scanning of displays in kiosks and stands in airports
and hotels indicated that generally only a small part of the
display space was used for books and that the offering consisted mainly of low priced books and pamphlets rarely selling for
more than 25 kopecks. It should, however, be noted that quite
a few works of belles-lettres are published in magazine form
and that such editions are staple items in the Soiuzpechat' outlets.

Special Bookstore Chains

There are a limited number of special distribution networks which are controlled either by other government agencies
or by individual publishing houses. The most notable of the
latter category are the bookstores of the Publishing House of
the Academy of Sciences and those of the literary fund of the
Union of Soviet Writers. Special network outlets specialize in
selling the production of the agencies or publishing houses by
which they are controlled and supplied directly. However, they
also offer a limited selection of other publications which they

receive from the Knigotorg system.

Retail Sales

Bookstores are responsible for practically all retail sales. This concentration on one channel of selling is in sharp contrast with the United States practice of utilizing additional means of distribution such as book clubs, direct mail, house to house salesmen and sales directly to schools and other institutions. The stores fall into several categories: general bookstores and stores which are specialized either by subject matter of books (for instance, political, technical and scientific, medical, books from satellite countries and books in minority languages); or by method of sales (for instance subscription or mail order sales). There seem to be very few second-hand bookstores. We visited bookstores of most categories in Moscow, Leningrad, Kiev, Pereyaslav-Khmel'nitsky, Sochi and Alma Ata and found them arranged in a rather standard pattern. The books were stored on book shelves or in cupboards along the walls more or less according to a prescribed basic classification: (1) social and political literature; (2) natural sciences; (3) technology, industry and transportation; (4) agriculture; (5) medicine; (6) education; (7) belles-lettres; (8) children's literature. In larger stores other categories were added, such as books in various foreign languages, translations, subscription editions, music and illustrated material such as postcards and posters. For identification the sections for each of these categories are marked by signs. In belles-lettres scanning of books on the shelves showed mainly the most recent production of contemporary literature, classics and translations of standard foreign works, with hardly any back-list titles published prior to 1960.

Except in a very few of the newer bookstores the public has no direct access to the books. Customers are separated from the wall shelves by counters, which often contain a display of books under a glass top. The sales personnel is located between the counters and the wall shelves.

83

In order to find out what titles are available the customers must depend primarily on oral information from the sales personnel; but they also have access to card indexes which list the books in stock and books forthcoming in the near future. Some bookstores also keep a calendar listing the daily incoming titles. In addition, annual catalogs (thematic plans) and other printed information on new or reissued books are accessible to the customers. Finally, there are supplies of postcards, which the customers can address to themselves, listing forthcoming titles which they wish to receive upon publication. However, only in a few cases did it seem that these sales helps were complete or kept sufficiently up to date.

Special Types of Bookstores

Deviating from the general pattern are the operations of the subscription bookstores (or subscription departments of general bookstores) and the mail order bookstores.

The subscription bookstores or departments handle only multi-volume works published over a period of months or years such as encyclopedias and sets of classics. Such editions are subscribed before publication and the store keeps a file of the subscribers and the books they order. Upon publication of each volume the customer is notified and picks up the books in the stores, unless he has requested delivery by mail. (In the subscription bookstore which we visited in Kiev, 30% of the orders were shipped by mail). When subscribing the customer has to pay in advance the price of the last volume. In addition he has to pay cash for each volume when delivered, either to the postman or in the bookstore. If he fails to pick up his subscription, he loses his payment for the last volume. The stores also have for sale single volumes to the extent that leftovers are available from cancelled subscriptions.

The mail order bookstores serve mainly rural areas with little or no access to local retail outlets. They sell through advertising in local newspapers and by mailing information to steady customers as well as to select groups of potential buyers such as scientists, industries, unions, etc. The mail order store in Kiev, which we visited, claimed an annual sale of 2,000,000 books, priced at 840,000 rubles. It had an inventory of 8,000 titles and made 311,000 shipments last year. The mailing list of steady customers included 2,500 for fiction alone and its correspondence and order department received 7,000,000 letters last year. Delivery was made C.O.D., postage being paid by the customer; and 80% of the orders are filled from stock.

In some cases bookstore sales are not restricted to the store itself. We saw many bookstands on the sidewalk in front of the stores. We learned that bookstores also frequently operate bookstands in factories, office buildings and cooperative farms, as well as in schools and other educational establishments at the beginning of the new terms. Bookstores sometimes use volunteers, particularly for the sale of political literature, who are recruited mainly from members of the Komsomol and similar groups. We were told in Alma Ata that the number of such volunteer workers in Kazakhstan was 4,500 and that they had sold 7,000 copies of books during the first six months of 1962. In that Republic use is also made of 65 bookmobiles which travel around the country selling directly to the public.

Kiosks are located at high traffic points in the streets as well as in hotels, airports and railway stations. There are many different kinds - from modern, glass-enclosed to open wooden stands. Only in the latter category has the customer direct access to the literature. In the others the magazines and books are kept inside and the sale is made through a window.

Book Promotion

Besides window displays of books and some special displays under glass on the sales counters, we found catalogs and other printed material available to the public as well as posters and announcements fixed to the walls. Some bookstores also maintain customer lists for mailing information to them. Besides these conventional activities bookstores occasionally organize special book drives such as book weeks, bazaars, lectures and the appearances of authors of new books in stores. These activities are supported by promotional campaigns using advertising, posters, radio broadcasts and volunteer workers.

Order and Supply System

Knigotorg and the other distribution networks, and not the publishers, are responsible for the absorption and sale of the publishers production. This procedure (using Knigotorg, the largest system, as an example) operates in the following manner. Knigotorg receives from all publishers in advance the annual "thematic plans" or advance catalogs, which contain information on publishing programs by author, title, book category, price, length and planned print order. This information and periodically issued "order blanks" are passed on to the bookstores which then make estimates of their potential sale of each book. On the basis of these estimates, Knigotorg places its orders with the publishers. In some cases the bookstore estimates received are changed upwards or downwards by the central Knigotorg administration. Publishers occasionally will disagree with the judgment of Knigotorg and will print more than ordered. If they do so, Knigotorg may or may not accept the surplus on a consignment basis.

Additional information on all publishing activities is supplied by the All-Union Book Chamber - the state publishing house for bibliography and statistics in Moscow - and supplemented by similar centers in all Republics. The Chamber issues many kinds of bibliographies, among them weekly and monthly catalogues of new or reissued books. These catalogues represent the nearest equivalent to weekly listings in the U.S. book trade journal, Publishers' Weekly.

Over or Under Supply

Since advance estimates or sales are subject to errors and since some publications which are pushed out in substantial quantities in the interest of the State have disappointing sales, surpluses develop in the Knigotorg warehouses or in the bookstores. In order to eliminate or at least to reduce such overstocks, reminders and new order forms are sent to bookstores and reorders encouraged. Exchanges of overstocks between bookstores are arranged by the local Knigotorg agencies. Further relief is sometimes sought by price reductions and the special display of such reduced price books in bookstores. However, such price reduction can only be made by Knigotorg for whole regions and not by individual bookstores. The last resort is pulping of definitely unsalable stocks. We were often told that overstocks did not present a real problem but many special displays of reduced price books in bookstores and considerable inventories in the central warehouse, in Moscow, gave us the impression that the number of books which must be pulped cannot be insignificant. On the other hand we were told repeatedly that many books are sold out quickly and reorders hard, if not impossible, to obtain. That seems to apply particularly to sets of books which are subscribed before publication takes place, but also to many other successful or popular books. The reason for this seems to be not only a shortage of paper and manufacturing facilities, but also a lack of flexibility of the whole centrally controlled system. It is difficult to obtain paper and press time beyond the initial yearly allocations, so that most reprints or reissues have to wait for inclusion the following year in new thematic plans, new approvals and new order estimates. This is in sharp contrast to the roughly 160,000 book titles held in stock listed in the Bowker annual Books in Print from which it is possible for American readers to order older titles through their bookstores.

Warehousing and Shipping

Knigotorg operates six large warehouses in Moscow and 25 warehouses outside of Moscow, of which 14 are located in the capitals of the several Republics. The largest of the 6 Moscow warehouses takes care of 60% of all books handled in the Moscow area. It receives books of an approximate value of 200,000,000 rubles per year and has a floor space of 28,000 square meters - 252,000 square feet. Knigotorg also operates reshipping points in the provinces and ships directly to approximately 100 large book shops. The total number of warehouses and shipping points is approximately 500.

The central warehouses receive books published by the various Moscow publishing houses directly from the printers and books published in the Republics from the Republic warehouses, which in turn also receive books published by Republic publishers directly from their printers.

In the central warehouse in Moscow, approximately 10% of the incoming books are put into storage. They represent stocks in excess of orders on hand, as a result of errors in Knigotorg estimates or intentional over ordering from the publishers. The stock is used for reorders, stimulated by the promotional efforts mentioned above, or by spontaneous demand from Knigotorg offices or bookstores. There are also showrooms on the premises for each major book category, in which samples of the books are displayed on racks and wall shelves and card indexes maintained with information on quantities and locations of the books in the warehouses. Here bookstore managers can inspect the books and place reorders. The warehouse stock is arranged in stacks on simple wooden bases on the floor and in rows numbered for identification.

The remaining 90% of incoming books is immediately processed for reshipment. The books arrive by truck, either in corrugated cartons with metal or cord strapping, or wrapped only in paper. The trucks are unloaded by hand onto skids, which in turn are moved by forklift trucks into big mesh wire cages of two basic sizes. Each shipping point has one or several of such cages. Except for an especially urgent case, the cages are emptied for shipment only when they are full, but we were told that it never takes more than ten days before that happens. At the time of shipment, the books are transferred from the wire cages into heavy waterproof shipping boxes, each the same standard sizes as the cages. The boxes are marked as to destination, sealed and loaded on trucks which transfer them to the railways where they are reloaded on flat cars. (Eight of the large containers go on a twenty-ton flat car).

Books which go into inventory are moved by elevator to a storage floor which is equipped with a conveyor belt from which they are unloaded onto hand-driven carts to be moved into their final location.

Knigotorg performs all of its functions (warehousing, shipping, promotion and selling) on a discount of 25% of the retail selling price, of which the central organization in Moscow retains 5% and 20% is passed on to its local agencies.

General Observations

It is difficult to find standards of judgment for a system with purposes in many respects so different from ours. Even if we disregard such basic differences of purpose and consider only the technical question of the most efficient and widespread distribution of books, the U.S.S.R. methods appear to have many shortcomings. Among the most obvious are the following:

The use of bookstore estimates for determining print orders, and sometimes publishing policy, cannot fail but to impede creative initiative in the publishing process. The retailer or his clerks can hardly be expected to have a proper judgment on the merits of new books, particularly on the basis of the scant information provided by the thematic plans, or in case of reprints based on his individual sales experience.

The many roadblocks and delays which are inherent in the bureaucratic procedures of the ordering system cannot provide a really effective and speedy supply.

The lack of modern mechanization and backwardness of operating systems in the warehousing and shipping process contributes to these deficiencies.

The lack of backlist titles and the long delays on reorders gives the book buyer access at any one time only to a small part of the literary heritage of the U.S.S.R. and of Russia's creative writing before the revolution.

The difficult access to books in bookstores is not inducive to the promotion of book buying and reading. It prevents people from browsing and makes the purchase of books a time-consuming and sometimes tedious business.

Last, but not least, the lack of newspaper, magazine and radio advertising keeps large segments of the public insufficiently informed about the world of books.

It is nevertheless remarkable that a system with these and other deficiencies has been able to provide a country as large as the U.S.S.R., with its problems of transportation and with a population which a few decades ago was mostly illiterate, at least quantitatively with reading matter on a very substantial scale.

****

(Libraries, which are an important element in book distribution, have not been discussed in this chapter because of the existence of two excellent recent books in English on this subject, Soviet Libraries and Librarianship by Melville J. Ruggles and Raynard C. Swank, American Library Association, Chicago, 1962; and Libraries and Bibliographic Centers in the Soviet Union by Paul L. Horecky, Indiana University, Bloomington 1959. The Ruggles-Swank volume, published in late 1962, is based on the visit of a group of leading American librarians to the Soviet Union in 1961 under the cultural exchanges program).

V. STATISTICS ON BOOK PRODUCTION AND PRICES

The U.S.S.R. is without question one of the two countries in the world producing the largest number of copies of books. The United States is the other. Which of the two countries produces the most book titles and the most copies of books, both in absolute terms and in proportion to population, are difficult questions to answer in view of differences in definitions and statistical systems. Nevertheless, in addition to describing the book output of the U.S.S.R., we shall in this chapter attempt to arrive at as close an approximation as possible to a valid comparison. It must be pointed out, however, that although the U.S.S.R. and the U.S.A. are the largest book publishing countries in terms of total production of copies, this is in part because they are the third and fourth most populous countries in the world. Several European countries do as well or better on a per capita basis.

Comparing book prices in the two countries is also difficult because the ruble is not a freely convertible currency directly comparable to the dollar; and thus the conversion ratio of 90 kopecks equals one dollar enforced on foreign visitors within the U.S.S.R. is not a useable standard of comparison. We have, therefore, attempted to relate book prices to the wage scales within the two countries, using as a measuring rod the number of hours and minutes of work required to buy books of various types.

Soviet Book Production Statistics

The U.S.S.R. has probably the most complete and elaborate system of statistics on book production of any country in the world. Certain information about each book must be printed in the book itself, including such basic statistical data as length, price and number of copies printed. Copies of each book, pamphlet, circular, magazine or newspaper must be sent to the All-Union Book Chamber of the Ministry of Culture which then develops the elaborate statistical compilations published in the

annual volume, Pechat' SSSR. In addition to statistics the
Book Chamber is also responsible for much of the bibliographic
work of the Soviet Union; our delegation had an interesting and
informative discussion at this organization in Moscow on both
subjects. The Pechat' for 1961, which is the basic source of
the U.S.S.R. book statistics quoted in this chapter, contains
20 elaborate tables on book publishing in the U.S.S.R. as a
whole, plus four or five supplementary tables for each of the
fifteen constituent Republics of the U.S.S.R. It should be
noted that all of these statistics deal with the production,
not the sale, of books. Information on sales is much more difficult to come by, and does not appear at all in the Pechat'.

Soviet Statistical Definitions

It is essential to a proper understanding of Soviet statistics on publishing to have a clear grasp of the definitions
on which these statistics are based. There are four major ways
in which these definitions vary from American and Western European practice. First and foremost, there is no differentiation
between books, pamphlets and leaflets. All publications of five
pages or more (and a few with less) are considered together as
books-and-pamphlets. This contrasts with the UNESCO recommended definition now being used in the U.S.A. which defines a pamphlet as being between five and forty-eight pages and a book as
being forty-nine pages or more, not counting the covers. Sec-
ondly, in the U.S.S.R. there is no clear definition of a published "title". Three entirely separate categories of publications are lumped together as "titles" in the U.S.S.R. statistics: (1) entirely new books; (2) substantially revised books;
(3) unchanged reprintings of old books. In the U.S. and most
European countries only new and substantially revised books are
included in the statistics of annual title production, and mere
reprintings are not so included. Thirdly, all books and pamphlets are counted in the U.S.S.R. regardless by whom published,
whether or not distributed through the book trade, and whether
or not carrying a price, including such printed publications as

administrative instructions, catalogues, patents, industrial
standards, descriptions of new inventions or new processes,
construction plans for buildings, teaching programs for schools
and other items of a similar nature for specialized audiences.
In contrast the United States book title statistics include
only books intended to be sold through the book trade; they do
not include local, state or federal government publications,
business and industrial publications and such items as industrial standards and patents. Fourthly, because it is a multi-
lingual country the U.S.S.R. counts as "titles" each year translations of the same book in as many as sixty additional languages. This sort of multiplication in the counting of titles
does not of course occur in the U.S.A. with its single national
language.

U.S.S.R. Book Production - Titles

As will be noted in Table 2 attached, the number of book
and pamphlet titles published in the U.S.S.R. increased by
about 50% from 1930 to 1961 and about 200% since the immediate
postwar year of 1946. However, in 1961 there was a slight fall-
ing off in the total number of titles to 73,999 as compared with
76,064 in 1960. One explanation we were given for this slight
reduction was the shortage of paper. Table 3 attached gives a
breakdown for certain years as between books and pamphlets
which carry a price and those which are distributed free. It
will be seen from this table that priced books and pamphlets,
now account for about two-thirds of all titles, and that priced
items have been increasing much more rapidly than free books and
pamphlets, the number which has remained relatively stable in
the past twenty years. The 24,476 unpriced titles in 1961 are
an impressive part of the title statistics but they accounted
for only about 8% of the total number of copies produced.

If we take the total of priced books and pamphlets as
the only figure comparable in any way with U.S. book title statistics, we get a figure of 49,523 books and pamphlets (new
editions, revised editions and mere reprintings) published in

93

the U.S.S.R. in 1961 compared with 18,060 original and revised editions of books of forty-nine pages or over in the U.S.A. book title statistics compiled by Publishers' Weekly. A more comparable figure for the United States might be the copyright registrations of books, pamphlets and leaflets for the year ending June 30, 1962 which amounted to 61,787. However, even this figure does not include many thousands of state, local and federal government publications which are rarely copyrighted. In 1960 there were over 13,000 state and local publications alone that the Library of Congress considered important enough to list in its Monthly Checklist of State Publications.

Thus it can be seen that no very close comparison can be made of U.S.S.R. and U.S.A. book title statistics - the definitions and the statistical systems are too far apart to make this possible. It is clear, however, that if the same definitions were used the U.S.S.R. would not be shown to publish more new and revised editions of printed publications of 5 pages or more than the U.S.A.

U.S.S.R. Book Production - Copies

Tables 2 and 3 attached also show the number of books and pamphlets produced in the U.S.S.R. in 1961 and selected earlier years. In 1961 the number of copies produced - 1,119,400,000 - dropped by almost 10% from the total of the previous year, a somewhat larger decline than took place in the number of titles.

Comparison of statistics on copies produced between the U.S.A. and the U.S.S.R. is in some ways a bit easier than comparison of titles. In counting copies the U.S.S.R. practice of classifying reprintings as titles and multiplication of editions through translations into the minority languages does not substantially affect the total. The other factors tending to increase the U.S.S.R. figures - such as the counting of pamphlets along with books in an undifferentiated total - do remain a problem. This is also true of the lack of coverage in the U.S. figures (which are compiled by the book publishing associations)

94

of governmental and industrial publications.

The published figures in the two countries on the number of copies produced or sold for 1961 are almost identical; and in view of the much more restrictive definitions and coverage of the American figures it can be said with confidence that considerably more copies of books (over 48 pages) were produced in the United States in that year than in the Soviet Union, both in absolute terms and on a per capita basis.

1961 Production

U.S.S.R. Books and pamphlets over 4 pages produced	U.S.A. Books over 48 pages sold, not counting municipal, state, federal government publications and industrial publications
1,119,400,000	1,113,400,000
Per capita: 5.55 copies	Per capita: 6.05 copies

UNESCO Statistical Standards

Within a few years it may be possible to make much more exact international comparisons of book, magazine and newspaper publishing output, not only between the U.S.S.R. and the U.S.A. but for many other countries as well. The General Conference of UNESCO meeting in Paris in November and December, 1962, considered for the first time the set of standard definitions for compiling national statistics on book, newspaper and magazine production which were drawn up by a committee of experts which met in Paris in April, 1961. This set of definitions is in the course of being officially recommended by UNESCO to the member countries of that organization, and seems likely to be widely adopted. Both the U.S.S.R. and the U.S.A. have indicated their intention of supplying UNESCO with publishing data on the basis of these standards in so far as possible.

Book Prices

Book prices throughout the U.S.S.R. are highly standard-ized on the basis of a list of maximum prices for various categories of books which has remained unchanged since 1950. In practice the ceiling prices in the list tend to be the actual prices. This price schedule is in terms of the length of the book measured by "publisher's sheets" (40,000 letters and blank spaces). A few examples may be given: books for primary schools - 1 kopeck per sheet; for secondary schools - 1.3 kopecks per sheet; for poetry - 5 kopecks; for pre-school children's books - 4.5 kopecks. In addition there is an extra charge allowed for bindings starting at 3 kopecks for paper covers. A check of prices in the books examined in bookstores and in the listings of books in publishers' catalogs indicated that this price list is rather rigidly followed.

Practically all of the Soviet publishing officials with whom we met made a point of emphasizing how cheap Soviet books were as a matter of deliberate government policy; and a number of them went on to indicate how expensive they considered American books to be. It is true that compared with prices for many other consumer goods - particularly food, clothing and house furnishings - the Soviet government has established a relatively low price scale for books. However, in terms of the wage and salary levels prevailing in the Soviet Union, books are on the whole no cheaper for the Soviet citizen than for his American counterpart. We had quite some difficulty in convincing our Soviet hosts of the validity of this point; but we believe we did make an impression with a comparison in terms of the purchasing power, expressed in books, of the wages of skilled printing craftsmen in the two countries. We chose printing craftsmen because they were a familiar part of the book publishing and manufacturing industry. The illustration would be equally valid if wages in other occupations were used.

We took as our example the wages of linotype operators and pressmen who earn a basic wage in Moscow and Leningrad which averages about 100 rubles a month for a 41 hour week or just under 60 kopecks per hour. In the United States the current basic wage scale (not counting overtime) for these two occupations is just over $3.25 per hour ($3.29 for linotype operators and $3.24 for pressmen). Table 4 attached shows the number of hours which Soviet and American linotypers and pressmen would need to work to earn enough to buy various categories of books. It will seem that in one of these categories - scientific books - the U.S.S.R. prices are very slightly lower in this comparison, but U.S. novels and encyclopedia volumes are much cheaper. Over the whole range of books, using this scale of comparison, U.S. prices are probably lower than in the U.S.S.R. For one thing, the Soviet Union does not have anything comparable to our inexpensive paperback editions, both originals and reprints, which account for almost one-quarter of the total number of copies of books sold every year in the United States. This comparison also ignores the question of quality of manufacture; by and large U.S. books have better printing, paper, bindings and illustrations.

Table 2

Production of Books and Pamphlets in the U.S.S.R.

	Titles	Copies	Average number of copies per title	Average length in printer's sheets*
1930	50,954	867,300,000	17,000	3.5
1938	40,336	698,600,000	17,300	5.7
1943	15,900	228,300,000	14,400	2.8
1946	23,368	467,887,000	20,000	6.8
1950	43,060	820,529,000	19,000	8.5
1956	59,530	1,107,486,000	18,600	9.5
1957	58,792	1,047,266,000	17,800	10.1
1958	63,641	1,103,200,000	17,300	10.3
1959	69,072	1,168,698,000	16,900	10.2
1960	76,064	1,239,600,000	16,300	10.1
1961	73,999	1,119,400,000	15,100	10.1

*A printer's sheet is an area equivalent to one side of a sheet of paper 60 x 92 centimeters - about the same number of words as a publisher's sheet.

Table 3

Production of Priced and Unpriced Books and Pamphlets in the U.S.S.R.

(All languages)

	Unpriced Books Titles	Priced Books		
		Titles	Copies	Value in New Rubles*
1940	21,530	24,300	338,200,000	--
1950	17,260	25,800	720,100,000	--
1956	27,914	31,616	977,200,000	340,560,000
1957	26,889	31,903	918,147,000	338,950,000
1958	28,023	35,618	983,618,000	380,917,000
1959	21,595	47,477	1,065,038,000	415,316,400
1960	24,815	51,249	1,090,005,000	427,341,300
1961	24,476	49,523	1,031,900,000	376,500,000

*Earlier years converted to new rubles.

Table 4

Comparison of Book Prices, U.S.S.R. and U.S.A.
(in money and hours of work)

	U.S.S.R.	U.S.A.
Scientific and technical books (averaging 400 pages)	1.60 rubles [1] 2.66 hours [3]	$10.00 [2] 3.08 hours [3]
Novels, hardbound	1.39 rubles [4] 2.31 hours	$ 3.78 [5] 1.16 hours
Novels, paperbound	--	$ .56 [6] .17 hour
Large Soviet Encyclopedia	4 rubles per volume 6.66 hours	--
Encyclopedia Americana	--	$10.67 per vol. 3.28 hours

[1] Average from August 1962 Leningrad bookstore catalog of forthcoming scientific and technical books.

[2] From average per page cost of 2.5 cents for over 400 scientific and engineering books published in 1961-62 by two leading U.S. firms.

[3] Hours of work required by linotypers and pressmen to purchase books at average hourly basic wage rates of 60 kopecks and $3.25 respectively.

[4] From average of 5 new Soviet novels in Novye Knigi for September 1962

[5] Hardbound fiction average in the 1961 Cost of Library Materials Index (Publishers' Weekly, April 23, 1962).

[6] Average prices of new titles in Summer 1962 issue of Paperbound Books in Print.

VI. FOREIGN TRADE

The foreign trade of the U.S.S.R. in publications and certain related fields has been a monopoly for over thirty years of Mezhdunarodnaia Kniga (hereafter referred to as M.K.), the All-Union Association "International Book". M.K. is under the U.S.S.R. Ministry of Foreign Trade. In addition to books, M.K. handles the export and import of newspapers, magazines, music, phonograph records, musical tape recordings, illustrations, postage stamps and foreign "rights" to Soviet publications.

In foreign countries M.K. operates through agencies such as the following two examples of several in the United States: the Four Continent Book Corporation in New York City, and Cross World Books and Periodicals, Inc. in Chicago. Through several hundred of these foreign agencies and also directly, M.K. distributes periodic advance announcements of new books and its other publications and products. The principal advance catalogue of books thus used by M.K. is Novye Knigi (New Books) the weekly publication of the All-Union Book Chamber in Moscow. We did not get into details of export financing in our discussions in Moscow, but other sources indicate that the terms of payment for shipments by M.K. to foreign dealers are quite flexible. In some cases the agents overseas may purchase materials from M.K. on strictly commercial terms, whereas in others liberal credit and even consignment arrangements may be made. Internally M.K. receives its books for export from Knigotorg, the book distribution system; and its magazines and newspapers from Soiuzpechat', the corresponding newspaper and magazine distribution agency.

In its import business M.K. seems to bring in books and magazines primarily for distribution to a few specialized libraries. Except for books published in Soviet bloc countries, which are sold in one bookstore in each of the very large cities, foreign books cannot be purchased by consumers in the Soviet Union. There is one limited exception to this general rule: perhaps two-hundred French titles, mostly classics and works by

French communists, were on display and could be purchased in a section of a small Moscow bookstore which we visited. This is a special reciprocal arrangement with Hachette, the French publisher and bookseller.

Foreign Trade Statistics

A review of Soviet trade statistics confirms the impression gained from discussions in the U.S.S.R. that M.K. attempts as far as possible to "break even" on its export and import business, especially with respect to trade with countries having "hard" or convertible currencies. There follow several tables translated from the official annual foreign trade reports of 1956, 1957 and 1961 (Vneshniaia Torgovlia Soiuza SSR). Tables 5 and 6 show that in both 1960 and 1961 the combined volume of Soviet exports of publications, stamps and motion picture films was almost 30 to 40% greater than Soviet import of such materials. However, this export surplus was entirely in the trade with Soviet bloc countries. In trade with the rest of the world, Soviet exports and imports of these three classes of materials are rather closely balanced. With respect to books and other publications alone, Tables 7 and 8 show that the Soviet Union is an increasingly large net importer from both Western Europe and the United States.

Tables 9 and 10 show the export and import figures for each individual country for the years 1955, 1957 and 1961.

One further category of Soviet foreign trade - printing equipment - rounds out the picture. Although equipment of this type is not the responsibility of M.K., the trade balance in this field may well be related by the Ministry of Foreign Trade to the balance of payments on publications and associated items. For printing and binding machinery the Soviet foreign trade figures for 1960 and 1961 given in Table 11 show that the U.S.S.R. is a heavy importer not only from East Germany but also to a substantial degree from Hungary, Rumania, Austria and Finland. In these two years no exports of printing machinery from the U.S.S.R. appear in the official trade figures.

The continuing imbalance in foreign trade of books and magazines with the United States and Western European countries seems to be a matter of concern to officials of M.K. and of the Ministry of Foreign Trade. Obviously efforts are being made to bring about a less unfavorable balance, and this may in part account for the stepping up of translation programs and the photo-offset reprinting of many English language technical books and magazines. It may also account for some of the obvious interest in increasing sales of Russian language and translated books in Western Europe and the United States.

Table 5

Exports of Publications, Stamps and Motion Pictures
(1,000 rubles)

	1960	1961
Soviet Bloc	13,971	14,741
Publications	9,302	11,122
Stamps	246	252
Motion pictures	4,423	3,367
Other Countries	3,272	3,374
Publications	1,373	1,688
Stamps	366	389
Motion pictures	1,760	1,558
Total	17,243	18,115
Publications	10,675	12,810
Stamps	612	641
Motion pictures	6,183	4,925

Table 6

Imports of Publications, Stamps and Motion Pictures
(1,000 rubles)

	1960	1961
Soviet Bloc	8,543	10,415
Publications	6,577	7,752
Stamps	312	466
Motion pictures	1,654	2,197
Other Countries	3,668	3,439
Publications	2,158	1,894
Stamps	0	6
Motion pictures	1,510	1,539
Total	12,211	13,854
Publications	8,735	9,646
Stamps	312	472
Motion pictures	3,164	3,736

Table 7

Exports of Books and Other Publications
(1,000 rubles)

	1955	1957	1961
Soviet Bloc	6,134	4,240	11,122
Western Europe*	206	232	735
United States	77	154	290
Other Countries	148	191	663
Total	6,565	4,817	12,810

Table 8

Imports of Books and Other Publications
(1,000 rubles)

	1955	1957	1961
Soviet Bloc	3,961	7,775	7,752
Western Europe 1/	238	839	1,165
United States 2/	142	281	423
Other Countries	22	46	306
Total	4,363	8,941	9,646

1/Western Europe:
    Austria
    Belgium
    Denmark
    Finland
    France
    West Germany
    Great Britain
    Greece
    Italy
    Netherlands
    Norway
    Sweden
    Switzerland

2/ Is is known that quite a few American books are bought in London and therefore the U.S. figure is understated.

Table 9
Exports of the U.S.S.R. of Books and Other Publications
(in thousands of rubles)

Soviet Bloc:	1955	1957	1961
Albania	56	49	65
Bulgaria	483	460	1,559
China	776	803	1,885
Cuba	--	--	117
Czechoslovakia	882	788	1,834
Germany (East)	662	474	1,234
Hungary	153	162	501
Korea (North)	917	270	551
Mongolia	135	167	312
Poland	1,575	652	2,070
Rumania	485	335	755
Vietnam (North)	4	48	190
Yugoslavia	6	32	49

Other Countries:			
Afghanistan	2	3	21
Argentina	4	3	5
Australia	-	-	38
Austria	29	10	15
Belgium	11	8	25
Brazil	3	0	40
Burma	7	7	9
Cambodia	-	-	6
Canada	-	-	48
Ceylon	-	3	6
Denmark	3	2	8
Ethiopia	-	1	1
Finland	32	29	65
France	49	59	241
Germany (West)	2	17	98
Ghana	-	-	12
Great Britain	37	60	150
Greece	2	5	10
Guinea	-	-	8
Iceland	1	0	3
India	26	49	75
Indonesia	2	9	22
Iran	4	15	23
Iraq	-	-	8
Israel	20	-	-
Italy	11	9	34
Japan	34	31	111
Lebanon	7	5	5
Mexico	-	-	15
Morrocco	-	-	8
Netherlands	8	9	30
New Zealand	1	1	4
Nigeria	-	-	4
Norway	3	4	4
Pakistan	1	1	1
Sudan	-	3	5
Sweden	8	10	41
Switzerland	11	10	14
Syria	5	4	7
Togo	-	-	10
Tunis	-	-	1
Turkey	1	2	2
Union of South Africa	4	0	0
United Arab Republic	1	25	13
United States	77	154	290
Uruguay	7	3	39
Yemen	-	-	3

Table 10
Imports of the U.S.S.R. of Books and Other Publications
(in thousands of rubles)

Soviet Bloc:	1955	1957	1961
Albania	1	6	9
Bulgaria	27	185	863
China	112	441	366
Cuba	-	-	-
Czechoslovakia	137	473	1,423
Germany (East)	3,453	5,408	1,987
Hungary	59	405	771
Korea (North)	8	15	48
Mongolia	1	2	3
Poland	124	507	1,610
Rumania	38	298	571
Vietnam (North)	-	3	58
Yugoslavia	1	32	43

Other Countries:			
Afghanistan	-	-	-
Argentina	-	-	6
Australia	-	-	7
Austria	8	275	33
Belgium	4	9	14
Brazil	-	-	5
Burma	-	-	2
Cambodia	-	-	1
Canada	3	1	23
Ceylon	-	-	1
Denmark	3	5	14
Ethiopia	-	-	-
Finland	2	3	32
France	39	98	223
Germany (West)	72	178	196
Ghana	-	-	-
Great Britain	80	178	383
Greece	-	5	21
Guinea	-	-	-
Iceland	-	-	-
India	3	7	19
Indonesia	-	1	1
Iran	-	1	6
Iraq	-	-	1
Israel	-	-	-
Italy	9	28	102
Japan	5	9	32
Lebanon	-	-	-
Mexico	-	-	8
Morocco	-	-	-
Netherlands	6	17	58
New Zealand	-	-	2
Nigeria	-	-	-
Norway	1	2	6
Pakistan	2	-	1
Sudan	-	-	-
Sweden	4	18	25
Switzerland	10	23	58
Syria	-	-	-
Togo	-	-	-
Tunis	-	-	-
Turkey	1	1	3
Union of South Africa	-	-	-
United Arab Republic	1	3	3
United States	142	281	423
Uruguay	-	-	7
Yemen	-	-	-

Table 11

Printing Equipment Imports of the U.S.S.R.
(1,000 rubles)

Country	1960	1961
Soviet Bloc	13,401	15,085
East Germany	11,333	11,850
Hungary	1,403	2,085
Rumania	665	1,150
Other Countries	857	935
Austria	673	668
Finland	184	267
Unspecified	27	107
Total	14,285	16,127

Our delegation was, of course, primarily interested
and specialized in book publishing and consequently our investigation of book manufacturing was not extensive. This
chapter is based on discussions and inspections at plants in
three cities and a visit to a regional supervisory office for
printing in Leningrad.

Organization of Book Manufacturing

The most common Soviet organizational pattern in book
manufacturing is to have these plants operate under the
regional economic councils. The two plants we visited in
Moscow and Leningrad were thus situated. Some publishing
houses have their own printing plants, but we saw none of
these. The third plant we inspected, in Alma Ata, was under
the Republic Ministry of Culture, an uncommon arrangement.

The regional economic council allocates publishers to
particular printing plants under its jurisdiction. The various printing plants cannot compete with each other on the
basis of price differentials since there is a standard nationwide scale for various types of work and length of print run.
This limits competition to service and quality of work. If
publishing houses are not satisfied with the work of one
plant, they can go elsewhere provided they can find available
facilities. It is usually more difficult for a publisher to
find unused capacity than for the printing plant to fill any
gaps in its production schedule resulting from the withdrawal
of a publisher.

Production planning in each plant is based on financial and physical quotas. A yearly contract is signed with
each of the several publishing houses for which work is done;
and a monthly plan is set up under each of these contracts.
The printing plant then makes up its own composite monthly
plan based on these contracts with the publishers. Publishing houses supply the paper and the binding materials; the

other materials are supplied by the printer. The publishers specify such details as the paper to be used, binding, design and type faces, and inspect the work while in process.

Each plant has its own planned budget, production quota and profit goal. If the production plan is exceeded or costs reduced, excess income will be earned by the plant and this excess is distributed (1) to the workers in social benefits such as vacation expenses, kindergartens and housing; and (2) as cash bonuses to the workers and the management. Workers can earn up to a maximum of 25% of the base salary in cash bonuses and the administrative and professional staff up to 40% of base salary. An additional maximum of 40% of base salary can be earned as rewards for suggestions adopted on new methods and new inventions. The director and the professional staff of the department of the regional economic council which supervises and directs the actual printing plants may also get bonuses for excess production in the plants.

If the plant or production quota is not fulfilled, there are no bonuses for the staff and the plant goes in debt to the industrial bank for the losses. If failure to meet the production quota is due to deficiency in management, the management will eventually be changed; if the management is not demonstrably inefficient, the production plan or quota will be adjusted downward.

When technical improvements are made in a printing plant and excess profits result, the excess profits for that year are used for the benefit of the plant staff and the management; however, the production quota for the plant is raised for the following year. The publishers do not share in the benefits by way of price reductions unless the whole nation-wide price scale is changed.

Wages, Deductions and Pensions

In the Moscow and Leningrad regions the base salary scales were as follows: typesetters, 90-100 rubles a month;

pressmen, 90-110 rubles; engravers, 150-170 rubles. The
minimum pay is 55 rubles for sweepers and the highest 170
rubles for engravers.

In the plant in Alma Ata, on the other hand, we found
the following higher base pay wage scales: engravers, 200
rubles a month; color pressmen, 180-200 rubles; ordinary pressmen, 150 rubles; bindery workers, 80 rubles; typesetters in
six grades ranging from 100-150 rubles; linotype operators
from 120 to 150 rubles; retouchers of offset plates, 200 rubles.

We were told that the maximum variation in the regional
schedules of wages in the U.S.S.R. was 10%, but the difference
between Alma Ata and Leningrad and Moscow as shown above seems
to be greater than this. At any rate wages in Alma Ata have
been set higher than in Moscow and Leningrad in order to
attract skilled workers to that developing area.

The basic work week is six days, seven hours a day
except for six hours on Saturday. Some employees engaged in
hazardous work may work somewhat fewer hours and this is also
true of employees 17 years old and those attending night
school. Overtime is permitted with the concurrence of the
trade union up to two hours maximum. The base salary for
workers is paid for meeting the production quota; quantity and quality bonuses up to 25% of base salary may be paid
for producing over the quota.

Income tax, and this is true throughout the U.S.S.R.,
is withheld from wages at the rate of 7% on the first 100
rubles a month and 6% more thereafter. Thus the top income
tax rate is 13%. We were reminded that under existing decrees
the income tax was going to be reduced the following month and
that by 1965 there would be no income tax. Shortly after we
left the U.S.S.R., however, it was announced that the scheduled income tax reduction for the fall of 1962 had been cancelled.

After the optional retirement age, workers who continue on the job may receive their retirement pay plus current salary. The retirement age also seemed to vary by

region. It was given as 55 for women and 60 for men in
Leningrad but five years less in each case in Alma Ata. Maximum pensions for workers who had received top salaries of
200 rubles a month would be 120 rubles per month. Minimum
pensions are 50 rubles per month.

Other Working Conditions

If workers wish to quit they can do so after two weeks
notice. There is not a great deal of inducement to shift
employment from one plant to another because the salary
scales and production quotas for workers are uniform within
the same region and do not vary too much throughout the whole
country. In addition, shifting jobs from one town or city
to another is difficult unless such a move is arranged by an
employer because of the difficulty of securing housing in
the new location. Reduction in the job classification of a
worker can only be made with the approval of the trade union;
the same is true of promotions. Reduction in job classifi-
cations is used as a disciplinary step only after other
efforts are made to solve the disciplinary case.

Depending on the job and skill classification of the
workers, vacations range from 12 to 24 days a year plus 8
legal holidays. This is also the vacation allowance for
management, professional and technical staff, except this
latter group may earn additional days of leave for overtime.

Supervisory Office for Printing of
the Leningrad Regional Council

In Leningrad, our delegation met with the chief of the
printing department (Poligrafiia) of the Leningrad Regional
Economic Council and several of his principal assistants.
We were given a general overview of the 16 printing plants
in Leningrad and the surrounding area, not all but most of
which come under the supervision of this central office.
With respect to the problems of further mechanization, however, all 16 plants look to this office for guidance.

Magazines and books are printed in eight plants in the

Leningrad area; three are specialized offset plants; one is
a plant specializing in lithography; one is a labeling manufacturing plant; one is a typesetting operation; and two are
small printing plants for supplementary work on labels and
advertising matter.

Annual production of all eight book and magazine
plants per year is 70 million books in hard covers; and 100
million booklets, paper-backed books and copies of magazines.
This makes Leningrad a major printing center, but not nearly
as large as Moscow. One single plant, Pechatnyi Dvor (see
below) produces annually over 50 million books in hard
covers and about 45 million booklets in a two-shift operation.

The total personnel of all sixteen printing plants is
about 12,000, 70 to 75% of which are women. About 10 per
cent of the staff of the printing houses is administrative
and professional, divided equally between the two. This 10
per cent does not include foremen, nor members of the central designing staff which numbers about four hundred for
all of the 16 plants. There is a total of about 600 foremen
in the 16 plants under the Leningrad Economic Council.

Moscow Plant No. 1

Our first plant visit was to Printing Plant No. 1 in
Moscow, which was founded in 1876. The "No. 1" is an arbi-
trary designation and has no relation to size or importance,
but this establishment does happen to be one of the largest
diversified printing plants in the Soviet Union. It is one
of the more than ten printing houses operating under the
Economic Council for the Moscow region. In addition there
are others under other ministries and organizations. This
plant produces for some 25 publishers almost all types of
printed materials: books, pamphlets, magazines, art materials, illustrations for books, calendars and color posters.
The daily capacity in two-shift operation is 75,000 hard-
bound books, 100,000 pamphlets or paperbound books and

100,000 calendars produced by letterpress and offset. Paper consumption is about 100 metric tons a day.

Production is divided into shops depending on the nature of the physical processes involved - composition, letter press printing; offset printing, gravure, pamphlets shop, bindery, machine repair, electrical shop, power supply and waste materials. In addition there are sections for planning, organization of labor, inspection, new equipment, accounts, supply, administration as well as the following chief officers: chief engineer, managing director, economist, deputy for management, technologists, chief designer, chief power engineer, dispatcher and daily production quota manager.

There are 2,500 total personnel in Moscow plant No. 1 of which administrative, technical and supervisory amount to 11%. Seventy per cent of the personnel in the plant are women and 65% of the management personnel are also women.

Our tour of the plant revealed a great deal of East German equipment throughout. The plant, a four-story old building, was extremely crowded and in poor condition. There was no mechanization of the flow of work with the exception of one small bindery line. Typesetting was by linotypes of Soviet manufacture plus a good deal of handsetting for complex work such as mathematical symbols.

The Pechatnyi Dvor Printing Plant in Leningrad

This was the second plant which we visited. Pechatnyi Dvor, which dates from a small beginning in 1829, produced books primarily but also a few magazines. The main building was constructed in 1910-1912 as an exact copy of a French plant in Paris. Books have been produced since 1910. The capacity is 160,000 hardbound books per day plus a similar number of pamphlets and paperbound books. Paper consumption is 100 metric tons per day. Letter press is used exclusively. Forty per cent of the production consists of textbooks; 30-35 per cent of political and Marxist literature; and the balance is fiction and technical and scientific books. The average print order is 275,000 copies, with a minimum of 200,000 copies for fiction and 160,000 copies for textbooks. The plant specializes in extremely long runs for 10 different publishing houses.

Two shifts are operated each day with a total of 2,400 employees. Observation indicated that a large majority of the employees were young women. Our tour of the plant revealed a fairly complete mechanized operation with much use of conveyors - a sharp contrast to the Moscow plant. A rough count of the presses indicated 32 flat-bed and rotary perfectors printing from sheets; and 13 rotaries printing from rolls. Most of the flat beds were of East German manufacture dating from 1957 and later. The rotaries with folders on the ends were all of Soviet manufacture dating from 1953 and later. Practically all of the equipment except the flat-bed presses, sewing machines and folders were of Soviet manufacture. Maximum size of the presses was 92 x 127 centimeters for flat-bed presses and 84 and 92 centimeters for rotary presses. East German equipment would probably not exceed 25-35%. There was no perfect binding equipment.

The Printing Plant in Alma Ata, Kazakhstan

This diversified establishment, the largest in the printing industry in Kazakhstan, produces magazines, posters, art work, calendars, and books by letter press and offset. It dates from 1947. The ten magazines produced in the plant range in circulation from 20,000 to 200,000 copies per issue. Average book edition size in the plant is about 25,000 with a maximum of 200,000.

There are 550 employees in this plant plus 200 additional employees who work on building construction including housing related to the plant. The operating schedule is two shifts a day on the standard six-day, 41 hour week.

Paper (2,500 tons per year) comes from Leningrad, the Urals and the Far East. The price of paper ranges around

20 kopecks per kilogram delivered, or 204 rubles a metric ton.

Sixty to sixty-five per cent of the employees in the plant were women, mostly of European extraction. Kazakh employees seemed to us to number no more than about 10% of the total. Forty-five of the employees were supervisory staff, including the director. The average age of the staff is very young, less than 30 years and only 10 persons employed are beyond retirement ages of 50 and 55 for women and men, respectively. The 200 additional building employees have constructed two 16-unit apartment houses for the workers in the plant and are now working on more apartments plus the reconstruction of the bindery building.

On our tour of the plant, we noted in the composing room 10 linotypes of Leningrad manufacture plus one old German machine. There seemed to be somewhat less hand-setting than in the other two plants, possibly because fewer scientific, technical and mathematical books were produced.

In the press room there were 11 flat-bed presses, mostly manufactured by the Sherbokoff plant in Rybinsk, dating from 1953-1960 plus one East German machine. All of the small color presses - 3 or 4 - were of German or Czech manufacture dating from 1955 to 1960. The flat-beds were operating at a rate of about 36 sheets a minute. One sheet-fed rotary was operating at about 2,100 per hour. The three German rotaries, sheet-fed, were operating at 5,500 sheets per hour on one-color work; these three presses were manufactured in 1955 and 1957. Three separate folders were all East German. There was one Sherbokoff rotary with folder on the end manufactured in 1954. There was also one Plausen East German rotary manufactured in 1955. In reply to a question as to why there were no Soviet-manufactured offset presses in the plant, the director indicated that such presses were scheduled to be received within the next year. In the bindery the nine sewing machines seemed to have been manufactured either in Kiev or Leningrad dating from 1957 and later.

We found the building itself to be very well laid out and uncrowded, but not nearly so mechanized, especially in the bindery, as the Leningrad plant. The construction, however, was modern - one and two stories with a good deal of natural light especially in the press rooms - orderly and clean.

Summary

Our general impression of book manufacturing based on these limited observations and discussions plus the examination of many books in bookstores may be briefly summarized. Machinery used is old fashioned by U.S. and Western European standards even when it is fairly new. This is particularly true of bookbinding. Some modern machines such as those for perfect binding seemed to be completely lacking in the plants we inspected, and we saw in the bookstores only a very few perfect bound books. There is little straight-line production, partly because many of the older plants are in multi-story buildings not adapted to modern layouts. All of this can easily be understood in terms of the lag created by wartime destruction and the emphasis on heavy industry at the expense of consumer products. In finished books the result is generally a serviceable product, but again one which is not up to American or Western European standards. Paper stock is not of first quality. Illustrations, and particularly color work, leave much room for improvement.

On the other hand, the management of the plants seem to be good and the working force - largely young women - diligent. The management and technical staff in the printing plants and publishers also seemed quite aware that the U.S.S.R. was lagging in the field of book manufacturing and were looking forward to installing more modern equipment and techniques. We were informed that a major interest of the Soviet delegation coming to the United States on the reciprocal visit in 1963 will certainly be in book manufacturing and modern printing and binding equipment rather than in publishing techniques.

There is one national government publishing house for belles-lettres (Goslitizdat) for the U.S.S.R. as a whole plus one in practically all of the constituent Republics. The Republic houses specialize in the language and the local literature of the region. Their output is fashioned to serve the state. From small beginnings these publishing houses have experienced rapid growth, the direct result of public demand plus targets set by the state. Fiction represents their major output. Then follows general literature, modern literary criticism, Russian and Soviet classics with world classics and other well established works of foreign literature in translation. They also issue literary magazines, literary newspapers and a relatively few children's books. Despite the growth of belles-lettres, the total output of this type of book is now only about 30% of the entire book production in the U.S.S.R. (318 million copies in 1961).

We visited three belles-lettres publishing houses. The central house in Moscow with its Leningrad branch is by far the largest. The Republic houses in Kiev and Alma Ata are smaller and are patterned on it. A comparison of the three follows (1961 data):

	Goslitizdat U.S.S.R. Moscow	Goslitizdat Ukraine Kiev	Kazgoslitizdat Alma Ata
Annual output in "titles"	375	229	283
Annual output in copies	42,807,000	4,614,000	4,368,000
Personnel	420	120	100

Each house conforms to the usual program of prefabricated publishing. Each house prior to December 1st issues its thematic plan of projected titles for the following year. Each house conforms to the universal pricing pattern. Each house hews to the line of issuing books which either serve the interest of the state or books that are politically safe and harmless. Each house operates with separate editorial boards for each type of literature - Moscow with 9, Kiev and Alma Ata each with

6. Each house has special characteristics that reflect the region. Kiev as the capital city of the Ukraine, publishes 98% of its books in the Ukranian language. The other 2% are in Russian. In Kiev we also found some of the best designed of any books on our visit. They were putting out very commendable products. Alma Ata by contrast did no publishing in Russian until this year when it issued 35 titles in Russian. Otherwise, its books were almost entirely in the Kazakh language, save for 17 books in the language of a remote section of the Republic. In 1913 Kazakhstan was 2% literate. Today they claim no illiteracy.

Of particular interest are the monthly and bi-monthly fiction magazines issued by the Moscow and Kiev houses, Moscow with 7, Kiev with 3. These magazines are the nearest parallel to our mass market paperbound books, despite the difference in format. In appearance they resemble somewhat the Atlantic, Harpers or Harpers Bazaar, but with inferior paper and covers. They contain, along with biographical data about the author, a complete novel, which may run in one or several issues. If the demand warrants, such a novel appears later in book form. Thus, initial publication of novels is normal in the pages of these magazines and not in book form. This is an old practice: the early chapters of Tolstoy's War and Peace first appeared in a magazine. The only important magazine which publishes reprints is Roman-Gazeta of Moscow which has a circulation of 500,000. Of these 380,000 are sold by subscription with the balance being sold in bookstores of kiosks.

The Moscow house is the central one in belles-lettres exclusively except for the publishing house of the Union of Soviet Writers. Its prime function is to publish Soviet and world classics or other already established literature. In addition it publishes magazines and issues annually books in translation from 40-50 foreign languages, with separate departments for Oriental, Latin American, European and other geographic subdivisions. We were furnished a complete

list of 58 books by American authors published in translation
by this house in the period 1945-1961. It will be noted how
few of these authors were still actively writing during the
past thirty years. The list and the number of titles for each
author is as follows:

Bret Hart (3)
O. Henry (3)
Theodore Dreiser (8)
Washington Irving (1)
Erskine Caldwell (1)
Fenimore Cooper (1)
Henry Wadsworth Longfellow (2)
Jack London (7)
Albert Maltz (3)
Frank Norris (1)
Edgar Allen Poe (2)
Mark Twain (8)

Walt Whitman (1)
Howard Fast (1)
Richard Hildreth (1)
John Reed (1)
Sinclair Lewis (2)
Upton Sinclair (5)
Harriet Beecher Stowe (1)
Ernest Hemingway (2)
Phillip Bonoski (1)
Jay Deiss (1)
Dorothy Parker (1)
Irving Stone (1)

The figures on sales of classics or established foreign
authors are impressive. Here we found among others Dickens in
30 volumes of 600,000 each, Mark Twain in 12 volumes of
300,000 each, Walter Scott - 20 volumes of 300,000, Tagore -
12 volumes of 100,000, Jack London - 8 volumes of 390,000,
Chekhov - 20 volumes of 100,000, Dostoyevsky - 10 of 300,000
and a recently-completed definitive Tolstoy in 90 volumes of
5,000 each. A set of Pushkin's works has reached a total sale
of 2,180,000 copies. (See also Table 12).

Two other special publishing houses which we visited
were related to belles-lettres - the Union of Soviet Writers
and the publishing house of the Hermitage Museum in Leningrad.

Union of Soviet Writers

The Union of Soviet Writers was founded by Maxim Gorky
in 1935. It is a self-ruled, non-party organization with a
platform of socialist construction and 5200 members. It has
60 branches throughout the U.S.S.R. and with its own publishing house, publishes in 60 different languages. It has an
annual output of several hundred titles, 17 literary newspapers and 16 magazines, the largest of which reaches a circulation of 560,000. The Union is governed by an elected board
of writers. It encourages new writers and protects the interests of its author members. Its profits go into a security

fund for the benefit of authors. The director referred to the Union as "a friendly cooperative of authors," as an instrument of encouraging new talent.

The Union's publishing house for belles-lettres "Soviet Writer" is the second largest publisher of this type of book in the U.S.S.R. - 395 "titles" in 1961 and 12,477,000 copies.

Hermitage Museum Publishing House

The publishing house of the Hermitage Museum likewise holds a special place. The Museum itself, originally the Court Museum, is some 200 years old, contains 1000 rooms, of which 400 are used for exhibit purposes, and compares favorably both in size and operation with any other museum in the world. It contains two-and-a-half million art objects, with some 8000 paintings, only 3000 of which are on exhibit. The Museum publishing house has been in existence for only four years. One of our delegation visiting the Museum three years ago found nothing other than poorly produced black-and-white reproductions. Today very fair reproductions are coming from the presses including the first of a five volume set which will contain reproductions of the great masterpieces of the Museum. The color work for this book, which was printed for the Museum in Czechoslovakia, is outstanding in production quality. The Museum publishing house was established to publicize its collections and has a program for bringing out scientific works, catalogues, reproductions of different art schools and guide books. As one of the only two publishing houses devoted exclusively to art publications, it too is unique in the U.S.S.R.

Table 12

Books and Pamphlets - Russian and U.S.S.R. Minority Authors
of Belles-Lettres by Dates Authors were Active
(All languages)

	Pre-Revolutionary Authors		Soviet Authors	
	Titles	Copies	Titles	Copies
1954	748	50,375,000	3,637	137,197,000
1955	798	54,092,000	3,857	148,536,000
1956	776	61,010,000	4,298	179,905,000
1957	700	48,310,000	4,666	198,886,000
1958	676	51,587,000	5,720	246,922,000
1959	742	48,716,000	6,169	251,130,000
1960	649	34,498,000	5,927	257,728,000
1961	523	29,100,000	5,658	224,100,000

IX.   SCIENTIFIC AND TECHNICAL BOOKS

The information presented in this chapter is based on meetings with the most important and representative of the large number of houses publishing scientific and technical books other than those described in Chapters X, XII, XIII and XIV. This chapter then must be recognized as illustrative rather than definitive.

1.   The Publishing House of the U.S.S.R. Academy of Sciences is the most important single source of original scientific and technical books. Its growth reflects the growth of the scientific and technical research programs administered by the Academy of Sciences. From 1950 to 1962 the total output of the publishing house almost tripled and in 1962 approximately 60 per cent of its publishing program was in book form. In 1961, 804 books and 76 journals were published.

The selection of titles is done with the help of the editorial council of the presidium of the Academy of Sciences whose members review all proposals to determine their scientific value for contemporary audiences. The annual thematic plan is also approved by the editorial council.

A major part of the book program is a by-product of research carried out by the various institutes of science, all of which, except those in chemistry and biochemistry, the publishing house attempts to serve. Some manuscripts prepared independently of research are accepted for publication. Other responsibilities of the publishing house include the popularization of science by books for general readers. For equally broad audiences there are three specific series for republishing the classics of science, general literature and fiction.

The publishing house has two printing plants, one in Moscow and the other in Leningrad. It also has access to an ample supply of paper.

2.   The Publishing Houses of the Academies of Sciences of the Republics. About twelve Republics have such houses

engaged in publishing books but only one, that of the Kazakh
SSR was visited.

The Kazakh Academy of Sciences Publishing House, although founded in 1946, did not begin its real growth until
ten years ago. The regular publishing staff is supported by
an editorial council of fifteen members of the Academy of
Sciences whose functions parallel those of the U.S.S.R.
Academy of Sciences Publishing House described above.

Its output has almost quadrupled in the past decade during which a total of 1,100 titles and 3 million units were published. More than 7,000 degree holding scientists in fifty-
four research institutes and establishments are its principal
source of monographs and reference books. Of its 1961 planned
production of 190 titles forty per cent were in the biological
sciences and medicine, more than twenty per cent were devoted
to mineral studies and geology, over thirty per cent in the
social sciences and humanities, and in physics and mathematics,
a new publishing area, only eight per cent. The balance might
be called miscellaneous. Actual production in 1961 was 61
titles and 154,000 copies.

The average printing of the 190 titles planned for 1961
was 1,500 copies, the smallest printing 500 copies, and the
largest (History of the Kazakh Republic) 20,000 copies. We
were informed that all of the authors were citizens of Kazakhstan but that eighteen per cent of them published in Russian,
a percentage stated to be the highest of any publishing house
in the Republic.

The selection of books, although largely the responsibility of the editorial council, is also made with the help of
other critics. Because all manuscripts come from staff members of institutes and are usually thoroughly reviewed before
submission a rejection is a rarity. On a smaller scale this
publishing house has a broad program similar to the publishing
house of the Academy of Sciences of the U.S.S.R. for it publishes folklore, dictionaries, documents and nine scientific

journals.

3. U.S.S.R. Committee for the Coordination of Scientific Research. In 1957 when a number of ministries were dissolved five large technical publishing houses were placed under the control of a predecessor organization of the Committee in an Association of Scientific and Technical Publishing Houses (ONTIZ). The Association has a staff of 3,000 of whom 1,000 have publishing responsibilities and 2,000 are employed in six printing plants. The subject areas covered are machine building, metallurgy, mining, gas and oil and food processing. Building construction is being added.

The committee has the management responsibility for overall planning, financial planning, including working capital and profits and printing schedules. Every effort is made to avoid duplication as well as to assure thorough coverage of all important subjects.

The selection of books appeared to be very well organized. Specific subjects are assigned to both experienced and new authors, sometimes as a result of overall planning, and often as a result of conferences during which prospective authors are identified. Superior books are sought as additions to the literature or to replace inferior books. Competition for acceptance is keen to the extent that only twenty per cent of the proposals are published. The general mission of each of the houses is to provide books emphasizing methods of preparing and producing materials and manufactured goods. Of 3,100 current titles approximately ninety per cent are original and the balance translations.

4. State Publishing House of Literature for Physics and Mathematics (Fizmatgiz). This house which is under the control of the Ministry of Culture was established in 1931 and has a branch in Leningrad with a total staff of 215. About forty-five editors devote their time to books in physics, mathematics, astronomy, mathematical statistics, theoretical mechanics and popular science. Another twenty-five editors

are assigned to dictionaries.

Approximately 125 original reference books and 25 dictionaries are published annually. Excellent advice is obtained from advisors and consultants. The average printing of a reference book is 8,000 to 10,000 copies, the minimum 3,000 and the maximum 20,000. For dictionaries the average is 8,000 copies and the maximum 75,000. Total output in 1961 was 191 titles and 6,380,000 copies.

5. The State Publishing House for Foreign Literature, established in 1946, is under control of the Ministry of Culture. The staff of 650 is assisted by approximately 2,000 contract personnel who are responsible for Russian translations of foreign books and journals as well as a major program of abstracts and journals. Unique in the world of publishing, this house has a major public library under its control. Thorough use is made of a scientific council of 100 members divided into working committees, most of which are concerned with pure and applied science. In addition, as many as 500 scientists offer suggestions or recommendations and visiting foreign scientists are frequently helpful. In 1961 this house published 359 titles in 6,891,000 copies.

The problem of selection is probably impossible to solve perfectly. After a book has been carefully reviewed by two specialists and chosen for translation, the quality of the translation and speed are essential for obsolescence is inevitable.

An extremely valuable service provided by this publishing house is a series of journals entitled "New Books Abroad". These journals provide reviews of foreign books, a list of books acquired and announcements of new Russian translations. It is reasonable to surmise that the series provides a feedback channel in support of the selection of books for translation.

6. Other specialized publishing houses. A great many

such houses exist but there was no opportunity to visit them or to determine their programs. Chapter VII of Gorokhoff "Publishing in the U.S.S.R." provides what is probably the best available, although not necessarily entirely up-to-date information in the English language. In the Russian language up-to-date lists of publishing houses and the yearly production of each appear in the annual Pechat' SSSR.

X.   TEXTBOOKS FOR ELEMENTARY AND SECONDARY SCHOOLS

It is extremely difficult for American publishers of school books or other instructional materials to visualize, despite its simplicity, the textbook publishing system of the U.S.S.R.   On the other hand, it was even more difficult for our delegation to try to explain to textbook publishing houses in the U.S.S.R. the complexities of textbook publishing for the fifty states of the U.S.A., each with its own educational system.

We visited three elementary and secondary textbook publishing houses in the U.S.S.R.: the State Textbook Publishing House (Uchpedgiz) of the Russian Republic (RSFSR); the Textbook Publishing House of the Ukrainian Republic (Radyanska Shkola) in Kiev; and the Textbook Publishing House (Kazuchpedgiz) of the Kazakh Republic in Alma Ata.   In addition we visited an eleven-year school in Moscow and another school in Sochi.

The 1961 enrollment in the general elementary and secondary schools (the 8 or 11 year schools) in the U.S.S.R. was 39,086,000.   It is for these students that the general textbook houses which we visited publish.   Textbooks for the 2,370,000 students in specialized secondary schools are published by other houses along with university level textbooks (see Chapter XII).   The students in trade schools (1,266,000 in 1961) also use books published by other organizations.

The educational system and textbook publishing in the Russian Republic will be described first because this Republic is not only the largest but also because the Russian Republic Uchpedgiz publishes the basic Russian language textbooks for the entire U.S.S.R.   These Uchpedgiz textbooks in Russian are used throughout the U.S.S.R. in schools in which Russian is the language of instruction and also are translated into other languages in the Republic textbook houses.

Curriculum and Basic Textbooks

The following is a brief outline of the basic course of study for the general elementary and secondary schools.

Children start to school at age 7 in grade one and in some cases continue in the general school to grade eleven. School is compulsory through the 8th grade, but it is planned to require 11 grades. Grades 9 to 11 are now optional, preparatory for admission to universities and higher education institutes. Labor training and work periods are part of the educational program in the upper years for the children who continue in the general eleven-year schools. Other children transfer to the specialized secondary schools or trade schools. There are also a growing number of boarding schools.

Uchpedgiz publishes only one book for general distribution for the use of the pre-school child. This is a sort of reading readiness book with a picture alphabet and parents who have children about to enter school are urged to buy this book and familiarize the child with it. (Other books for young children, such as picture books, are produced by the children's publishing houses, Detgiz and "Children's World").

In the first grade, four books are used, two of which are devoted to the alphabet and the Russian language. The third is a beginning reader, and the fourth a numbers book, or the beginning of arithmetic. Approximately 3,500,000 copies of each of these books are produced by Uchpedgiz every year.

In the second grade, three books are used, two again dealing with the Russian language and grammar slightly advanced above the first grade books, and the third book a continuation of arithmetic.

In the third grade, similar books to those in the second grade are used, but slightly advanced.

In grade 4 the same arrangement of two language books, one reader and an arithmetic are used to which is added a natural science book. Toward the end of the 4th grade a new reader is included which contains short sketches of Russian history.

In grade 5, instruction begins to be divided more definitely into subject matter areas: in addition to language, reading and arithmetic, biology and geography are added. Physics is introduced in the 6th grade and chemistry and mechanical drawing in the 7th grade. Mathematics, developing into algebra and geometry begins in the 6th grade.

Also at the 5th grade level, instruction in a second language begins. It is obligatory for a second language to be started by each student when he enters the 5th grade in the Russian schools. Theoretically the child may make a choice of a second language. However, only the larger schools offer courses in more than one foreign language. Once a student selects his second language in the 5th grade, it is obligatory for him to continue the study of that language as long as he continues in the school. If he wishes to change to another language, he may do so with special permission but is quite likely to have to transfer to another school and this practice is obviously discouraged. In 1960 the enrollment in various languages was: German, 8,249,000; English, 4,530,000; French, 1,049,000; and others, 8,000.

For the 5th grade in English there is a paperback book of 40 pages called "Speak English, It Is Easy", as well as a paperback "Merry Rhymes for Little Ones" which is a book of nursery rhymes such as Little Boy Blue, Polly Put the Kettle On, and Pat-a-Cake, with music. The 1961 Uchpedgiz edition of "Speak English, It Is Easy" sells for 15 kopecks and the press run was 136,000. "Merry Rhymes for Little Ones" sells for 11 kopecks. Its 1961 press run was 100,000 copies. "Think and Answer" is another widely used paperback; it is a combination workbook, quiz book, and crossword puzzle book of 52 pages which sells for 10 kopecks. The press run of the 1960 edition was 95,000.

For the more advanced classes in the teaching of

English in the 9th and 10th years there is a hard-cover book, "The Way to Spoken English". The 1961 edition sells for 32 kopecks and the press run was 106,000. These books are followed, among the students continuing English, by selections from American and English literature including items such as The Magic of Oz (The Wizard of Oz) and abridged editions of Shakespeare, A.J. Cronin, and other authors. A systematic study of Russian literature begins at the 9th grade level. From the foregoing it is apparent that in each grade from the 5th to the 11th an average of about 8 textbooks are used.

Uchpedgiz in Moscow - the Basic Schoolbook Publisher

The State Textbook Publishing House of the Russian Republic (Uchpedgiz) operates under the Ministry of Education of the Russian Republic (RSFSR). However, in addition to serving all of the schools of the RSFSR, this publishing house also serves "Russian schools" in all the Republics of the Soviet Union. The Ministry of Education also is responsible for the Children's Literature Publishing House (Detgiz).

With a mere 80 to 85 basic textbook titles, an unstated number of which are reprints or revised editions, the educational publishing house of the Russian Republic planned to print this year (1962) a total of 190,000,000 books for schools or about 70% of all schoolbooks in the U.S.S.R. One hundred and forty million of these were to be for Russian schools of the U.S.S.R. and the balance were for schools in which Russian is the second language; i.e., for areas where other languages - Ukrainian, Uzbek, Kazakh - are the native tongues. In 1961 the actual production of this house was 784 titles of all kinds and 172,346,000 copies.

Uchpedgiz produces books for approximately 40,000,000 children aged 7 to 17, 33,000,000 of whom are in the Russian language schools and 7,000,000 in schools where Russian is the second language. This publishing house also produces instructional materials for the teacher training institutions

and maps, charts, and workbooks (a new and developing field
in U.S.S.R. publishing). Uchpedgiz uses annually about
70,000 metric tons of paper to produce, in round numbers,
250,000,000 books and magazines.

Publications for Teachers and Teacher Training

The teacher training institutions for which Uchpedgiz
publishes instructional materials are of two types: (a)
teacher training colleges, which would be similar to what we
in the U.S.A. formerly called "normal schools"; and (b) pedagogical institutes, which would be similar to our teacher
training institutions like George Peabody, or perhaps our
graduate schools of education. Textbooks for higher education - i.e., for universities, technikums, etc. - are produced by other publishing houses (see Chapter XII).

Although the number of textbooks published by Uchpedgiz is quite limited, with approximately 85 different titles
produced annually, there is a wide variety of other titles
primarily for teachers and for teacher training so that the
total number of titles produced in 1961 was 784. Of the 20
professional magazines for teachers which this house issues,
one is designed for teachers in the first four grades and it
has a regular circulation of 600,000 copies.

The other 19 periodicals relate to the specialized
subjects taught above the 4th grade. One is for those
teachers who teach English and other foreign languages. The
periodicals sell for an average of 10 kopecks per copy. Maps,
charts, and all forms of visual aids for the classroom or for
the teacher are included in the number of "titles" involved
in the total production of Uchpedgiz.

Distribution of Textbooks

The educational publishing houses are not concerned
with the distribution of the books they publish. Textbooks
are distributed in the same way by Knigotorg as are the books
of other publishing houses (see Chapter IV). Unlike the
usual practice of free schoolbooks in the United States,

elementary and secondary textbooks must be purchased by
parents in the U.S.S.R. Schoolbooks are put on sale at the
bookstores and in the kiosks. Also for a couple of weeks at
the beginning of the school year the community bookstore
frequently sets up a branch kiosk in the school itself. The
prices are the lowest of all book prices, however. Revisions
of textbooks are not encouraged, and in fact are discouraged
for the lower grades because parents with more than one child
wish to pass on the books to the younger members of the family.

Textbook Writing and Editing

Teachers and professors, specialists in their respective fields, prepare the original manuscripts for textbooks
on the basis of course outlines. Sometimes the author is
given an "order" to prepare the book, in which case it is
automatically accepted for publication. In addition the
textbook publishing houses conduct competitions for the preparation of texts which are announced in the pedagogical
magazines. Usually four prizes are offered: a first and
second prize and two consolation prizes. The publishing
house establishes a jury composed of 7 to 13 highly qualified
specialists. The number of entries in these competitions
usually is small, ranging from 7 to 20 submitted manuscripts.
Members of the jury are paid for examining the manuscripts
and writing critiques. Each contestant, regardless of whether
he wins a prize or not, gets paid for the cost of typing the
manuscript, postage and other expenses. Otherwise the contestant enters the competition at his own risk. Out of the
two top awards one is selected for publication but the runner-
up also gets a reduced royalty. If a publishing house
"orders" a textbook - i.e., invites an author to prepare a
textbook - then it takes the risk of getting a satisfactory
manuscript. Royalty scales for textbook writing and other
types of writing are discussed in Chapter XV.

The salaries of textbook editors in Uchpedgiz in Moscow range from 130 to 170 rubles a month. Proofreaders are

paid an average of 100 rubles a month. Uchpedgiz doesn't
operate its own printing plant but contracts for the production of books with about 65 different printing plants. Most
of the textbooks are hard-bound, though there are some
paperbound editions. Only 2,000,000 workbooks are now produced annually, but workbooks are now considered to be promis-
ing teaching tools and their use probably will be expanded
significantly in the coming years. A Russian language workbook is now in preparation and will soon be published in an
edition of 350,000 to 500,000 copies. Uchpedgiz does not
publish books in languages other than Russian but its Leningrad branch publishes small editions of a few books in 9
minor languages used in the extreme north of the Russian
Republic.

Textbook Publishing House Radyanska Shkola in Kiev

The educational publishing house for the Ukraine in
Kiev (Radyanska Shkola) in many ways is quite similar to the
educational publishing house in Moscow, though it produces
fewer copies of each book published since there are only
about one quarter as many students in the elementary and
secondary schools of the Ukraine as there are in the Russian
Republic.

Materials published by this publishing house are designed primarily for use in the schools using the Ukrainian
language, most but not all of which are in the Ukrainian
Republic. Books published include elementary and secondary
school textbooks, professional books for teachers, and some
higher education textbooks. Also four journals and one newspaper are published for teachers. The journals deal with pre-
school education, general education, literature and reading,
and language instruction for all grades.

This publishing house publishes 83 book titles for
the first four grades, which is considerably more than are
published in the RSFSR. The total press run of these 83
titles is approximately 11,000,000 copies per year.

134

The Russian language almost automatically becomes the second language taught in the schools of the Ukraine as well as in other Republics where the native tongue is not Russian. The child is given the "opportunity" to start to study Russian as a second language at the second grade level if the parent requests it, and we are told that practically all parents do so request. A third language is offered to the children, and, in fact, is almost obligatory beginning at the 5th grade, just as a second language is offered in the schools of the RSFSR at the 5th grade. We were informed that in the Ukraine 35-40% of the students start English at the 5th grade and about 30% German, with French the third most popular choice. Spanish is now about to be introduced, and there are plans to introduce Chinese instruction in a few schools. For grade five up and for teachers this publishing house produces approximately 43,000,000 books per year, bringing their gross press runs to approximately 54,000,000. In 1961 the actual count was 899 titles and 54,190,000 copies. Most of the printing of the textbooks is done in offset, with only a minor portion in letterpress.

There are approximately 33,000 elementary and secondary schools in the Ukraine and over 400,000 teachers. Twelve thousand of these schools cover only the first four grades. In the Ukraine at present attendance at school for only the first 8 grades or approximately age 15 is compulsory, but the future objective is to go to 11 grades as in the Russian Republic.

The curriculum of the schools in the Ukraine is essentially the same as in the other parts of the U.S.S.R., but Ukrainian authors are used in the preparation of textbooks in the Ukrainian language. All textbooks in the first four grades for the Ukrainian schools are written from scratch by Ukrainian authors except for arithmetic books, which are translations of the Russian language textbook. From grade 5 up translations of the Russian language textbooks produced

in the RSFSR are used with only such regional adaptations as
may be necessary for books dealing with such subjects as
geography and nature. In certain fields, of course, textbooks may be entirely different, as in the case of Ukrainian
literature, Ukrainian language and history of the Ukraine.
Some books are published in Hungarian for the Hungarian-
speaking minority, as well as books in German, English and
French for foreign language students. It is doubtless because of the additional language that this publishing house
produces many more titles of textbooks than does the publishing house of the RSFSR.

Our visit to Radyanska Shkola in Kiev was with the
director, the editor-in-chief and 12 department heads. The
publishing organization consists of 16 separate editorial
boards including the following: Russian literature, Ukrainian literature, foreign literature, history, foreign languages, geography, biology, chemistry, physics, mathematics,
maps, professional literature for teachers and special
schools, art, technology, visual aids, and Hungarian textbooks. Each editorial board has a chief and 5 to 8 employees.
There are also, of course, regular staff departments such as
production, finance and supply. The total staff is 314 persons including the employees in a small printing plant for
professional publications which are produced in small press
runs. The long press runs of textbooks are produced in the
printing plant of the Ministry of Culture.

Textbooks are sold through Knigotorg as in the Russian Republic. Authors of textbooks, as in the RSFSR, are
academic specialists in various institutions of higher learning and teachers in the elementary and secondary schools,
employed on contract or as the winners of competitions. This
year there was a competition for a new textbook on the Ukrainian language. Also recently textbooks for the first four
grades were revised because of the new laws relating to the
elementary school curriculum. Ordinarily, however, text-

books are not revised very often.

Schoolbook Publishing in Kazakhstan

In Alma Ata, the capital of the Republic of Kazakhstan, we met with the director of the textbook publishing
house, Kazuchpedgiz. This publishing house was established
about 20 years ago, but the present director has been in
office for only about a year. Unlike the Russian and Ukrainian situation, educational publishing in Kazakhstan is under
the Ministry of Culture; but the textbooks produced are in
accordance with specifications issued by the Ministry of
Education. This publishing house produces elementary and
secondary textbooks and some university-level textbooks,
primarily in the Kazakh language. It also publishes in the
Uigur language and books in the Russian language for teaching Russian in schools where Kazakh is the native tongue or
language of instruction.

In the Kazakh language schools there are said to be
10,000 teachers in the first four grades. In Alma Ata, the
capital itself, there are six special boarding schools which
teach in the Kazakh language in addition to a number of day
schools teaching in Kazakh. Recent rapid increases in the
population of Alma Ata and some other areas of Kazakhstan
because of the "virgin lands" agricultural program have been
made up primarily of people from east of the Urals, and therefore the number of schools in Alma Ata using Russian as the
principal language of instruction is now much larger than
the number of schools teaching in the native language.

There are 8 titles of books used in the first and
second grades, 6 titles in the third grade, 9 titles in the
4th grade, 7 titles in the 5th grade, and 8 titles in the
6th grade. In all Kazakh language schools the Russian language is taught beginning at the second grade. Other foreign
languages are usually started in the 5th grade. After Russian English is the most popular language, followed by German and French. A small amount of Arabic and Chinese is also

taught in some of the schools.

The required amount of schooling is now to be extended from the present 8 years to 11 years. Emphasis in 1962 is on the creation of textbooks for the 8th grade. In 1963 this publishing house will emphasize texts for the 9th grade, and the textbook program required by the extension of the school program to 11 years will be completed by 1965. As in the RSFSR and the Ukraine, competitions are held to select authors for new textbooks for the revised educational program. This textbook house publishes no journals or newspapers, but the Ministry of Education itself publishes a few magazines and a newspaper for teachers in the Kazakh Republic.

Approximately 40-45% of the elementary and secondary textbooks of this publishing house are translations from the Russian language. These translations are principally for use in the higher grades in standard subjects such as arithmetic. The goal for 1963 is to produce 144 basic textbooks as well as 50 titles of professional books for teachers and some supplementary textbooks. The textbooks in the Kazakh language used in the first four grades are usually produced in editions averaging 150,000-200,000 copies each. In 1961 the production of this house was 249 titles in 6,864,000 copies, requiring the use of more than 1,500 metric tons of paper. All printing is done in the printing plant of the Ministry of Culture in Alma Ata which we inspected and which is described in Chapter VII. The price for elementary and secondary textbooks ranges from 8 to 15 kopecks per copy.

Some of the university textbook titles deal with mathematical analysis, optics, pedagogy, and physics. The teacher training institutes in the area are devoted to the training of teachers who will teach in the Kazakh language; however, the local university gives teacher training courses in the Russian language as well as in Kazakh.

Textbook editors are paid a minimum of 100 rubles a month as their basic salary. Royalty rates of 300 rubles per author's sheet (about 16 pages) were said to be paid for writing textbooks, which is higher than the current scale in the Russian Republic (See Chapter XV). Translators are paid by the amount of translation done rather than on a monthly salary. The working hours in the publishing house are the standard 7-hour day for five days plus six hours on Saturday.

Table 13 which follows gives a breakdown of textbook production of all kinds in the year 1961.

*****

(Note: In talking to textbook and other publishers we found that they believed English to be the foreign language being studied by the largest number of students in the schools at the present time. However, the official published statistics for 1960 cited on page 66 show that German is still the most frequently taught foreign language.)

Table 13

Production of Textbooks, Programs and Guidance Literature
in the U.S.S.R.
(All languages, 1961)

	Titles	Copies
Total	18,778	364,578,000
Textbooks (excluding correspondence)	6,016	297,368,000
Primary and secondary schools	2,709	264,010,000
Technicums, etc.	314	5,637,000
Higher education	2,530	20,050,000
Trade schools, etc.	70	2,515,000
Enterprise course network. etc.	393	5,156,000
Textbooks (correspondence)	3,895	15,355,000
Technicums, etc.	907	4,183,000
Higher education	2,553	8,685,000
Enterprise course network, etc.	374	1,179,000
Programs and guidance literature	8,867	51,855,000
Party schools	101	2,077,000
Primary and secondary schools	3,084	27,116,000
Higher education	1,718	7,399,000

Note: Subtotals do not add in some cases in the source,
table 14 of Pechat SSSR, 1961.

Detgiz is the larger of two publishing houses devoted exclusively to publishing children's literature in the entire U.S.S.R. It, like the Educational Publishing House (Uchpedgiz), operates under the auspices of the Ministry of Education of the RSFSR. The other general children's book house is "Children's World", under the Ministry of Culture of the U.S.S.R. Detgiz produced 586 titles in 99,995,000 copies in 1961 and "Children's World" only 116 titles in 11,889,000 copies. Some of the other Republics also have children's publishing organizations as departments of general publishing organizations as, for example, in the Ukraine and in the Georgian Republic. The total output of children's books by all publishing houses in the U.S.S.R. in 1961 was 2,718 titles in 166,700,000 copies.

Our delegation had a meeting with the assistant director of Detgiz and several members of his editorial staff at the House of Children's Books in Moscow because the Detgiz premises were disrupted by construction work. The output of Detgiz is limited exclusively to books for children; no magazines and no textbooks are produced. The smallest editions are generally about 200,000 to 500,000 copies for titles directed to the 2-6 year age group. The largest editions run to about 1,500,000 copies. The following are some typical prices and edition sizes of Detgiz books which we inspected. Small paperback pamphlets are priced at about 10 kopecks each. Books similar to the "Golden Books" published in the U.S.A. in hard, paper-covered bindings average about 44 kopecks each in price. A hard-bound supplementary reader was 74 kopecks. A six-volume edition of Fenimore Cooper, hard cover, sold at about 1 ruble 40 kopecks per volume by subscription and was produced in an edition of 300,000 copies. A collection of 20 volumes of adventure stories, approximately 500 pages in each volume, was also

produced as a subscription book in an edition of 300,000
at a price of 11 rubles 50 kopecks for the 20-volume set.

Children's books in sets are quite popular in the
U.S.S.R. Examples are the "Golden Library" of Russian
classics, and sets of books on the theatre, art and one on
poetry. A special department of Detgiz translates books
into Russian from the Republic languages and from foreign
languages.

Although Detgiz is the main publishing house devoted
exclusively to children's literature, other publishing houses
in the U.S.S.R. also publish a few books for children. For
example, the belles-lettres publishing house in Moscow,
Gozlitizdat, publishes a number of books for children annually. The Youth Guard Publishing House, which is connected
with the Communist Party Pioneer and Komsomol movements,
publishes 12 magazines and newspapers for young people as
well as books. There is also a multi-volume children's
encyclopedia which is produced by the publishing house of
the Academy of Pedagogical Sciences.

Detgiz has a branch publishing house in Leningrad
and also operates two printing plants - one in Moscow and
one in Leningrad. The entire output of the Children's Publishing House is sold through Knigotorg, the book selling
system, just as all other books are distributed. On the
whole, the variety and the general appearance of most of the
books we examined in the House of Children's Books was quite
good. The printing, binding and art work did not usually
come up to the American level, but the display of books was
quite impressive.

One of the popular current children's titles which
we purchased in a Moscow bookstore is Mister Twister, a well-
illustrated book, attractively printed on good paperstock,
in the "School Library" series, published by Detgiz. This
is a children's story about a rich American capitalist,
owner of factories, newspapers, steamship lines and banks.

He smokes cigars and is very fat. He reserved four cabins
for his family on an ocean liner from New York to Leningrad.
Four giant porters were required to carry the 24 pieces of
luggage into the hotel. The family noticed to their horror
a black-skinned man descending the staircase. The rest of
the story is rather easy to surmise. After a dream ending
on a nightmarish note, the capitalist and his family are converted to the tolerance of the U.S.S.R. Despite being warned
that their neighbors to the right would be Chinese, to the
left, Malayans, on the floor above, Mongolians, with mulattoes
on the floor below, the converted Mister Twister says, "We'll
take the rooms. Let us have the keys." This book was first
published many years ago; the 1962 edition we saw had been
printed in 300,000 copies.

XII.   TEXTBOOKS FOR HIGHER EDUCATION

Three years ago the U.S.S.R. Ministry of Higher and Specialized Secondary Education established the publishing house "Higher Schools" and assigned to it a five year plan. The formidable task of the staff of 200 is first to meet the immediate needs of students and second, to anticipate the needs of future students.   A major responsibility is to provide instructional materials for students of science and technology, as defined by the Soviets, but not medicine.   The students to whom the publishing program is addressed are classified "secondary" which is the equivalent of technical institutes in the U.S.A. and "higher", or university level. This publishing house was established for the purpose of eliminating duplication and conflict in textbook materials, but both continue at the present time.

The same basic textbooks are used by all students, and for correspondence students study guides are also provided. Textbooks, supplementary textbooks and study guides make up the publishing program for original works.   In addition, some textbooks and supplementary textbooks are translated from foreign languages.   Unlike many publishing houses this one has its own printing plant.

The procedure leading to publication of a new textbook can be generalized.   After an appropriate authority has decided that a new book or a replacement is needed an author is selected.   He may offer his prospectus unsolicited or may be commissioned, but in either event it is usually necessary to start with a prospectus.

Members of the publishing house who serve as editors are qualified specialists in the various disciplines who usually have had about two years training in publishing.   The discipline editors guide each project through preliminary reviews which lead to a contract.   The author who is an experienced teacher, but may be a member of an Institute staff, is given all possible assistance including paid free time to develop and complete the manuscript. Throughout all stages of development of each manuscript the quality of its content and methodology is painstakingly reviewed by appropriate critics, before the manuscript receives its final clearance from the high committee of the Ministry. There is at all times a high degree of control over the author's performance, a practical necessity for his book becomes the textbook for the course throughout the U.S.S.R.

Because this publishing house has its own printing plant, production time is relatively short. We were informed that a book of 320 printed pages could be manufactured in about five months.

Reflecting nationwide or area needs as well as the national interest special and urgent textbook programs are undertaken. As an example there was cited the field of agriculture. In April 1962 fourteen textbooks were commissioned, and in August the manuscripts were ready for production. The authors were granted paid leave, and provided with every conceivable form of assistance and critical guidance. Seven of the books had single authors, several had two authors and in no case more than four or five. In the latter instance one author managed the project.

In general there is but one textbook for each course. Occasionally more than one is available, which in effect means a single alternate. There seemed to be recognition of the necessity of not freezing textbooks indefinitely, especially when the professors agree a course must be modified. Some of the Republics develop indigenous textbooks as well as publish translations from Russian. Conversely, some textbooks are translated into Russian from the languages of the Republics.

In 1961 the "Higher Schools" publishing house issued 639 titles in 11,402,000 copies.

Although we were informed that textbook publishing was being centralized in this publishing house, it is obvious that this process is far from complete. Among the other sources of textbooks and supplementary text materials for higher education are the following:

1. Publishing House of Foreign Literature, the entire output of which consists of translations. Of its current offerings a substantial part is made up of translations of leading standard textbooks from the U.S.A. as well as from Great Britain. The selection is uneven; some of the best textbooks from the West have been overlooked and some of the inferior have been translated.

2. Publishing houses of the U.S.S.R. Committee for Coordination of Scientific Research: probably engaged in some textbook publishing, subject to the control of the Ministry of Higher Education Five Year Plan.

3. State Publishing House of Literature for Physics and Mathematics: more than 50 textbooks per year, including many translations from U.S.A., Great Britain and Germany.

4. Presses of the major universities: faculty members publish instructional materials which may have only local use. No first-hand investigation of university presses was made by our delegation.

5. Publishing House of Foreign Languages. Its principal effort is addressed to foreign audiences but this publishing house also publishes textbooks in foreign languages for Soviet students.

6. Publishing houses of the several Republics. A limited amount of original textbook publishing is done in the larger Republics such as the Ukraine. In the case of the Ukraine most of the textbooks at this level are published in Russian but occasionally they appear in Ukrainian. We also had an opportunity to discuss an even more limited program in Alma Ata, the capitol of Kazakhstan.

XIII. ENCYCLOPEDIA AND DICTIONARY PUBLISHING

Encyclopedias

The information on the publication of encyclopedias
has been drawn principally from a conference at the State
Scientific Encyclopedia Publishing House of the U.S.S.R. in
Moscow. This publishing house, established in 1949, operates
directly under the Council of Ministers of the U.S.S.R.

The permanent staff of 400 includes 300 editors and
proofreaders. To support and extend its work the permanent
staff uses a comprehensive network of outside editorial boards.
The 400 members of the outside boards are also members of the
various academies or otherwise distinguished authorities.
Almost all the advisors are from the Soviet Union but some
assistance is obtained from other countries.

The largest single project of this house has been the
second edition of the Great Soviet Encyclopedia, published
over a period of eight years, the work of 16,000 contributors
who prepared 97,000 articles. Each article underwent extensive critical review before publication in order to ensure
authoritative and concise contributions. Emphasis is placed
on short articles; a contributor of five articles of 1,000
words each receives more compensation than he would for one
article of 5,000 words. An additional control is achieved by
paying identical fees to editors, to authors and to critics
for each article. The fee to each is from 150 rubles to 300
rubles per author's signature or approximately 40,000 letters
or spaces (about 16 average pages). A third edition of this
work will be started in another two or three years and will
again be published a volume at a time over a period of five
years.

Major works already published include:

1. Great Soviet Encyclopedia, 2nd edition (1949-1958)-
51 volumes, plus an index of two volumes. The subscription
price for volumes 1-15 was 5 new rubles each, for subsequent
volumes, 4 rubles, and the complete set, 215 rubles. This

edition was published over a period of eight years and is being kept up to date by supplementary annual yearbook of which five have been published. 200,000 sets were printed.

2. Short Soviet Encyclopedia, 3rd edition - 10 volumes plus a single volume subject and name index. 300,000 sets printed.

3. Biographical Dictionary of Men Prominent in Science and Technology - 2 volumes - 1952 and 1953. 700,000 sets printed.

4. Housekeeping Handbook - 2 volumes. 550,000 sets printed.

5. Great Medical Encyclopedia, 2nd edition, Volumes 1-26 (early volumes published by Medgiz).

6. Concise Encyclopedia of Atomic Energy - 1 volume.

7. Guide to Leningrad - 1 volume.

8. U.S.S.R. Economic Life: Events and Facts, 1917-1959 - 1 volume.

9. Dictionary of Music - 1 volume.

New titles only partially available at the present time include:

1. Short Chemical Encyclopedia - 4 volumes planned at 3 rubles, 50 kopecks each. 1 volume published - 85,000 printed.

2. Geographical Encyclopedia - 4 volumes. 2 volumes published.

3. Theatre Encyclopedia - 5 volumes. 1 volume published.

4. Encyclopedia Dictionary of Physics - 5 volumes. 1 volume published.

5. Soviet Encyclopedia of History - 15 volumes. 2 volumes published.

6. Short Literary Encyclopedia - 6 volumes. 1 volume published.

7. Encyclopedia of Philosophy - 5 volumes. 1 volume published.

Additional publications planned for the future include:

1. Encyclopedia of Pedagogy.

2. Encyclopedia of Art - (to follow the pattern of the "Encyclopedia of World Art" by McGraw-Hill, New York, and the Instituto per la Collabarozione Culturale, Rome.)

3. Cinema Dictionary in two volumes.

4. Economic Encyclopedia.

5. Encyclopedia of Modern Technology.

6. Encyclopedia of Automation and Electronics in four volumes.

7. Encyclopedias of Continents, such as Africa, in two volumes and others in one volume.

8. Various indexes.

All of the multi-volume works are published one volume at a time over a period of months or years and are subscribed to in advance. This contrasts with the current American practice of publishing multi-volume encyclopedias in complete sets. The method of subscription and the system of distribution have been described in Chapter IV.

Since 1949 a total of 92 volumes have been published and 22 million units printed in 15 plants. About 2 million units have been exported to 50 countries and there are 3,000 subscribers of the various offerings in the United States. The current yearly paper allotment for the publishing house is 6,000 metric tons.

The only children's encyclopedia is not published by this organization but by the publishing house of the Academy of Pedagogical Sciences. Five volumes have been published and five more are planned in printings of 500,000.

The publishing house will accept commissions for articles in foreign language encyclopedias or will arrange for articles to be prepared by authors selected by foreign publishers. Copy will be supplied in Russian subject to an agreement that the translation and/or adaptation be approved prior to publication. Foreign publishers are expected to pay fees identical with those paid to their own authors.

Dictionaries

No visit was made to a publishing house exclusively concerned with this responsibility. There are many sources of dictionaries but the most important single source is probably the State Publishing House of Dictionaries under the Ministry of Culture, now twenty-five years old. Bi-lingual dictionaries in various Soviet and minority and foreign languages are published. In 1961 the output of this house was 46 titles in 1,669,000 copies.

XIV. TRANSLATIONS

The publication of translations is a large and important part of the U.S.S.R. book industry. Indeed, the Soviets can justly boast that they produce far more translations annually than does any other country. They have organized systematically for large-scale production of five kinds of translations:

1. Translations from foreign languages into Russian.
2. Translations from Russian into foreign languages.
3. Translations from Russian into the minority languages of the U.S.S.R.
4. Translations from minority languages of the U.S.S.R. into Russian.
5. Translations from minority languages into other minority languages.

Two large houses under the Ministry of Culture are chiefly responsible for translations of the first two types, respectively, The Publishing House of Foreign Literature (Izdatel'stvo inostrannoi literatury) and The Publishing House of Foreign Languages (Inogiz). Translations into the languages of the minority Republics of the U.S.S.R. are usually done in the Republic publishing houses. Most of these translations are from the Russian language; annually about 30% of the total of publications in minority languages are translations of Russian books (in 1961 it was 5,234 translated titles out of 18,598). A large part of such translations consist of books and pamphlets on political and social subjects. By contrast very few scientific and technical books are translated into minority languages, because Russian is the all-union language of science and industry.

In 1961, 9,819 translated books and pamphlets of one kind or another were published in the U.S.S.R. A tabulation by kinds of translation is given in Tables 14, 15 and 16.

The Publishing House of Foreign Literature is a large

151

organization by any measure. It publishes annually scores of
books translated from thirty foreign languages of seventy
countries, but chiefly from English, German, French and
Spanish - with English representing about 25% of the total.
In 1961 this house published 359 translations in 6,891,000
copies, with an average printing of over 19,000 copies. It
publishes chiefly scientific, social and political works and
foreign belles-lettres. Most of the translations from English
are of scientific and technical books, and about 60% of these
are from U.S.A. (See Table 17). In addition, it publishes
about twenty monthly and bi-monthly periodicals in science
and technology, each containing translations and reviews of
foreign periodical literature in its particular field. It
also issues a series of four journals entitled "New Books
Abroad," each of which covers a broad related field of science
or technology and contains reviews and critical annotations
of new foreign books in its area.

This publishing house also has administrative responsibilities for the large All-Union State Library of Foreign
Literature in Moscow, and it publishes a number of periodic
bibliographies compiled by this library.

This house has representatives in twenty-two countries
which review as many as 50,000 new books annually. These
representatives select the most important new titles, buy
copies in local bookshops and dispatch them to headquarters
in Moscow by air mail. It has 650 full-time staff employees,
and about 2,000 specialists who translate and edit on a fee
basis. Its editorial program is carried on under the direction of a 150-member Council of Advisors, and it has editorial
boards in eighteen major subject areas.

The Publishing House of Foreign Languages is another
very large establishment. It translates annually some 600
books into foreign languages, almost all from Russian and
largely into English, French, German and Spanish. In 1961
this house published 564 titles in 11,846,000 copies, or an

average printing of over 21,000 copies. Approximately 25%
of the books were in the English language. Most are political
and social works and fiction. Not many scientific and technical books have been so translated, but the number is increasing each year. Most of this production is exported outside
the U.S.S.R. through the M.K. organization. Domestic distribution is through Knigotorg.

This house has a total staff of 700 full-time employees,
most of whom are "editorial workers." The director expressed
some curiosity about mechanical translation in the U.S.A.,
but he obviously had little confidence that machine translat-
ing could be effectively developed in terms of either literary
or economic performance.

Although these two major "central" publishing houses
have primary responsibility for publishing translated literature, several other houses produce many translations in their
areas of special interest. For example, many translations
from the English of scientific and technical books are published each year by the State Publishing House for Physics
and Mathematics (Fizmatgiz, under the Ministry of Culture),
by the Publishing House of the Academy of Sciences, by the
technical houses under ONTIZ (about 300 titles annually), by
the several university presses and by the many specialized
"Institutes" of higher learning. Also each of the specialized
publishing houses for medicine, geography, law, music, etc.
publishes translations of foreign books in its area of interest.

In addition, the Publishing House of the Ministry of
Higher and Specialized Secondary Education (Vysshaia Shkola)
has embarked on a sizable program for the translation of
college textbooks into foreign languages. The director
stated that in the coming five-year period his house and the
Publishing House of Foreign Languages will produce a total of
at least 400 Russian college texts in English, French, German
and Spanish editions for export by Mazhdunarodnaia Kniga.

"We hope you will like them," he said pointedly.

Several of the publishing houses of the minority Republics also publish good numbers of translations, but most of
these are, of course, translations from Russian into the
minority languages. Apparently the Republic houses produce
only a few translations from their languages into foreign
languages. For example, with respect to the approximately
4,000 titles in the Ukrainian language published annually by
the Ukrainian Republic houses, about 30% of the total number
of copies are translations, of which the great bulk are from
Russian. Of original works written in this large Republic,
about 80% of the copies are in the Ukrainian language, only
4% in "foreign" languages for minorities living within the
Republic, for school use and for export outside the U.S.S.R.
through Mezhdunarodnaia Kniga. This year the latter category
will include three technical books published in English for
export only.

It is difficult for the outsider to understand just
how all these many programs are organized into a systematic
and coordinated national pattern, but it must be said that
all of them taken together add up to a very impressive and
effective blanket operation.

It is interesting to note that translators are well
compensated in the U.S.S.R. and that as a class they enjoy
a relatively high professional standing. The independent
translator can copyright his work and enjoy thereunder the
same rights as an original author, and 60% of the author's
royalty scale. Staff translators in the main two houses are
well paid. For the translation of scientific works, they
receive 92 rubles per author's sheet. For fiction they
receive 100 rubles per sheet. Skilled translators can finish
from two to five sheets per month, and thus earn from 184 to
560 rubles per month. (By comparison a compositor in a
printshop in Moscow has a base salary of about 100 rubles per
month and an engraver 150-170 rubles per month.)

It is also interesting to note that under the Soviet law a copyright is not infringed by publication of a translated edition, and as noted above copyright in a translated work is held by the translator and not by the original author. Further, it is significant to note that while authors writing in the Russian language cannot under the law receive royalties on translations of their works, authors of original works in the minority languages do receive royalties on translations into Russian. Obviously this double-standard arrangement has a double purpose: to encourage the widest possible use of Russian as the all-union language of the U.S.S.R. and not to seem to oppress the rights of minorities.

In the translation of belles-lettres from English, fiction titles are predominent, with a scattering of poetry, drama and criticism. Of U.S. authors, one finds in bookshops everywhere translations of several favorites among our classical writers - Jack London, Mark Twain, O. Henry, Fenimore Cooper, Harriet Beecher Stowe and Bret Harte. More modern and contemporary U.S. authors are sparsely represented by an odd assortment, including Sinclair Lewis, Hemingway, Steinbeck and Caldwell, along with Albert Maltz and Mitchell Wilson. The total list is limited and not at all representative of contemporary U.S. fiction. Tables 18 and 19 list the most popular U.S. and foreign authors translated in the U.S.S.R. These tables are here reproduced by permission from an article "American Books in Soviet Publishing" by Melville J. Ruggles, Slavic Review, October, 1961. This excellent article is highly recommended to all who want a good review of its subject.

In contrast to the situation in belles-lettres, translations of contemporary U.S. scientific, technical and medical books are available in large numbers in all the larger general bookstores in the cities of the U.S.S.R., and these translations represent a good percentage of the total titles available in the specialized technical bookstores. Table 20 also

reproduced from Ruggles, gives some interesting statistics
on numbers of titles and copies published in the U.S.S.R. of
translated U.S. books (other than belles-lettres) by categories.

Table 14

Book and Pamphlet Translations in the U.S.S.R.
by Language Groups
(Includes priced and free)

	1956	1957	1958	1959	1960	1961
Total	9,515	8,814	9,559	9,965	10,405	9,819
Into Russian	1,883	2,200	2,577	2,744	2,780	2,480
From minority	709	857	1,125	1,072	950	919
From foreign	1,174	1,343	1,452	1,672	1,830	1,561
Into minority languages	6,639	5,601	5,904	6,252	6,294	6,181
From Russian	6,010	4,890	5,007	5,252	5,329	5,234
From minority	232	256	223	291	331	396
From foreign	397	455	674	719	634	551
Into foreign languages	993	1,013	1,078	959	1,331	1,158
From Russian	933	942	951	849	1,209	1,038
From minority	47	52	77	81	88)	120
From foreign	13	19	50	29	34)	

Table 15

Book and Pamphlet Translations in the U.S.S.R.
from Foreign Languages
(Includes priced and free)

	1956	1957	1958	1959	1960	1961
Total	1,584	1,817	2,176	2,420	2,498	2,154
From Chinese	86	103	139	220	111	72
From English	485	515	559	648	835	737
From French	241	239	231	235	251	201
From German	212	259	351	374	398	315
From other languages	560	701	896	943	903	829

Table 16

Books and Pamphlets - by Language
(Includes priced and free)

	1958 Titles	1959 Titles	1960 Titles	1961 Titles	Total Copies
Russian	45,312	49,333	55,337	53,489	879,700,000
Minority languages	16,628	18,119	18,709	18,598	198,800,000
Foreign languages	1,701	1,620	2,018	1,912	40,900,000
Total	63,641	69,072	76,064	73,999	1,119,400,000

Table 17

Translation of Complete Books in 1962 Catalog
of the Publishing House of Foreign Literature

		Country of Original Publication			
Category of Books	Total	USA	UK	"Socialist Countries"*	Other
Scientific and technical	133	62	30	22	19
From English	104				
From German	15				
From French	8				
From Spanish	0				
Other languages	9				
Belles-lettres, history, social science, etc.	137	16	12	49	60
From English	29				
From German	19				
From French	14				
From Spanish	13				
Other languages	62				
Grand total	270	78	42	71	79

Year of Publication of Originals

1961 - 16   1958 - 48
1960 - 82   1957 and older - 45
1959 - 79

*Albania
 Bulgaria
 China
 Cuba
 Czechoslovakia
 Germany (East)- All Berlin titles assigned to East Germany
 Hungary
 Korea
 Mongolia
 Poland
 Rumania
 Vietnam
 Yugoslavia

Table 18

Most Popular Foreign Authors (Belles-Lettres)
in U.S.S.R., 1918-57, Translated and Published in
Five Million or More Copies

Author	Titles and Editions	Copies	Languages*
Jack London	662	18,588,000	32
Victor Hugo	362	13,184,000	45
Jules Verne	277	12,831,000	23
Hans Christian Andersen	221	11,880,000	35
Honore de Balzac	201	10,105,000	17
Mark Twain	241	9,415,000	25
Theodore Dreiser	120	8,525,000	12
Guy de Maupassant	282	8,350,000	16
Emile Zola	186	7,770,000	16
Charles Dickens	188	7,619,000	18
H. G. Wells	184	6,360,000	16
Romain Rolland	180	5,786,000	21

*Languages of the U.S.S.R. into which these works were
translated.

Table 19

The Soviet All-Time Best Seller List
of American Authors (From 1918 to July 1, 1959)

Authors	Titles and Editions	Copies (in thousands)	Languages*
Jack London	691	20,416	32
Mark Twain	256	10,926	25
Theodore Dreiser	133	9,531	13
Upton Sinclair	249	4,167	15
James Fenimore Cooper	81	4,055	12
O. Henry	122	3,991	8
Bret Harte	41	2,026	11
Albert Maltz	23	1,650	8
Harriet Beecher Stowe	49	1,646	18
Mitchell Wilson	13	1,115	3
Erskine Caldwell	12	1,112	2
Edgar Allan Poe	20	1,029	3
Sinclair Lewis	36	996	2
John Steinbeck	12	835	6
William Saroyan	8	815	3
Henry W. Longfellow	18	672	6
Washington Irving	9	499	3
Ernest Hemingway	17	487	7
Walt Whitman	15	281	2
Robert Sylvester	2	255	1
Sherwood Anderson	12	233	1
Langston Hughes	9	214	3
Ray Bradbury	1	165	1

*Languages of the U.S.S.R. into which these works were
translated.

Table 20

Publication in U.S.S.R. of American Works in Fields Other
Than Belles-Lettres During Postwar Period, 1946 to April,1959

Field	Titles and Editions	Copies
Social sciences (political science, sociology, economics)	159	3,300,000
Natrual sciences	313	2,600,000
Technology, industry, transportation, communications	326	1,400,000
Agriculture	41	252,000
Health and medicine	27	222,000
Literary criticism, linguistics, and art	15	373,000
Total	881	8,147,000

Royalties to authors in the U.S.S.R. are established
by decrees of the Council of Ministers of the several Republics. The most important of these decrees are those of the
Russian Republic which contains about 60% of the total population of the U.S.S.R., and a considerably higher percentage
of book publishing operations (see Table 22).

The scale of nonfiction royalties in the Russian Republic was significantly changed on March 29, 1962, by Decree
No. 326 "On Royalties for Political, Scientific, Production-
Technical, Training and Other Works of Literature." The
scale of royalties on fiction, however, remained unchanged on
the basis of a 1960 decree. The 1962 and 1960 scales of
royalties for various types of books are shown in Table 21.

Royalties Prior to 1962

In general the royalty scales provide for a specified
payment for each "author's sheet", which is 40,000 letters or
spaces in print - or roughly 16 pages of an average book.
Prior to the 1962 decree the author was paid this specified
amount per author's sheet (or major fraction thereof) for the
first "normal printing", and a declining percentage of this
amount for each subsequent "normal printing." The declining
scale was 60% for the 2nd and 3rd "normal printing;" 50% for
the 4th; 40% for the 5th; 30% for the 6th; and 20% for the
7th and over. For example, under the old scale the "normal
printing" of a university-level textbook was considered to be
25,000 copies; and the base rate of royalties was 150-250
rubles per author's sheet, depending on the quality of the
manuscript. Thus, if an author produced a textbook of this
type which was 20 author's sheets long and of the highest
quality, and if the initial edition was 40,000 copies, he
would have received royalties of 8,000 rubles (20 x 250 x
1.60 = 8,000). On larger initial editions or reprintings he
would have received a declining scale of royalties for each

additional "normal printing" or fraction thereof. For an initial edition of 100,000 copies, for example, he would have received 15,500 rubles.

Changes in the 1962 Decree for Nonfiction

Under the 1962 scale of royalties the "normal printing" concept is, as a practical matter, eliminated for most types of nonfiction books, and the author is paid on a flat scale. As indicated in Table 21, the "normal printing" is eliminated entirely for theoretical science literature, popular science literature, industrial and technical literature, textbooks and translated scientific works. For most fiction, poetry and children's literature the "normal printing" has been considerably increased over the 1958 level.

In addition, for textbooks and study aids for university-level and secondary-level general educational and vocational-technical schools, the new decree makes still further changes. The Ministry having jurisdiction now determines the maximum length for each specific textbook and the author is paid for a manuscript of that maximum length regardless of the actual size of the manuscript which is accepted. This change was made to reduce the financial incentive to the padding of manuscripts. Thus, under the new decree the author will ordinarily receive considerably reduced royalties. This may be demonstrated by using the same example cited above. If the maximum size of the textbook were set at 20 author's sheets and if payment was again made at the maximum rate of 250 rubles, elimination of the concept of a "normal printing" in an initial edition of 40,000 copies would in itself cut the royalties to 5,000 rubles or five-eights of the amount which would have been paid under the old scale (20 x 250 = 5,000). The author would get the same for a printing of 100,000 copies, less than a third of the amount which would have been paid under the old scale.

Comparison with the United States

It is obviously rather difficult to compare the royalties received by Soviet authors under the official scale and those received by American authors under typical publishing contracts. In general, however, the Soviet scale may be more generous for books having a very limited sale (5,000 copies or less) since the minimum basic royalties are paid on the first printing regardless of size and whether or not the books are actually sold. On the other hand, for books which sell from 10,000 copies upward the American royalty rates probably return a much higher income to the author because the usual practice in the United States is to increase the rate of royalty after the first 5, 10, or 15 thousand copies. In addition the Soviet author rarely receives royalties on translated editions in other countries because the U.S.S.R. is not a member of any international copyright agreement (See Chapter XIV). To revert to the hypothetical case previously used to illustrate the Soviet scale, a university-level textbook of 320 pages selling in the United States for $6.50 and printed in an initial printing of 40,000 copies would return to the author a total of $33,000 to $34,000 on the sale of the first printing and 95¢ per copy thereafter for several years. A college textbook with a first printing of 40,000 would probably sell 100,000 to 120,000 copies before revision, returning to the author total royalties from $80,000 to $115,000. This compares with the maximum of 5,000 rubles which would be paid to the Soviet author for such a textbook. The dollar and the ruble are difficult to compare in terms of purchasing power, but some indication of Soviet wage scales is given in Chapters V and VII.

Reduced Royalties to Heirs

Under Soviet law royalties received by the heirs of authors are also established by the decrees of the various Republics and the U.S.S.R. itself. (The U.S.S.R. copyright law provides that the term of copyright for most literary works is the life of the author plus 15 years.) Until 1957 the heirs of all authors received the same amount of royalties that the authors themselves would have received if alive. In 1957, 1958 and 1959 this scale was reduced in the Russian Republic by a series of steps to set royalties to heirs at 50% of the scale for living authors. In 1961 this 50% scale was extended by a federal decree to the entire U.S.S.R. In the decree of March 20, 1962, the Russian Republic reduced the scale of royalties to the heirs of authors of nonfiction works to 20% of the scale for living authors and applied this 20% retroactively. Thus in the Russian Republic the heirs of authors of nonfiction works received 20% of the current royalty scale whereas the heirs of authors of literary and dramatic works receive 50% of the current scale.

Advances on Royalties

The 1962 decree of the Russian Republic specifies the maximum amounts which may be paid to authors as advances on royalties. Prior to this decree it had not been the usual practice for publishing houses to grant such advances although it was permissible to do so. In the March, 1962, decree the maximum advance on royalties was again specified as up to 25% of the minimum scale but payment was still left to the discretion of the publishing houses. It remains to be seen whether in practice advances on royalties will be paid more frequently than in the past.

Summary

In summary it may be said that the royalties paid in the Soviet book publishing industry are set by statute or decree and are much less directly related to the volume of sale of individual book titles than is the practice in Western Europe, the United States and other major publishing countries. Under the Soviet system the author tends to be paid primarily in terms of the length of the manuscript, the quality of the work as determined by the publishing house, the importance of

the category of the book in the judgment of the state and the
economic requirements of the author. A major difference exists
between royalties payable for literary works and for nonfiction, both to living authors and to their heirs. Presumably
the higher literary scale is justified on the grounds that
writers of fiction, poetry, dramatic and musical works are
usually dependent upon their writing as a livelihood; whereas
the writer of nonfiction tends to be a salaried professional
worker. There is much less direct relationship between the
public acceptance of books, as indicated by their sale, and
the economic return to the author than is the case in most
countries outside the Soviet bloc.

Table 21

New and Old Scales of Author's Royalties (RSFSR)

Type of Literature	Normal Size of Printing (1,000 copies)		Rates per Author's Sheet (rubles)	
	1962 scale	1960 scale	1962 scale	1960 scale
Fiction, belles-lettres	to 100	(15)	150-400	(Same)
Poetry (per line)	to 50	(10)	7- 20	(Same)
Popular science literature for children	to 150	(15)	150-300	(100-300)
Children's literature, prose	to 100	(100)	250-400	(200-400)
Children's poetry (per line)	to 150	(50)	14- 20	(7- 20)
Translated fiction, belles-lettres, prose	to 100	(None)	100-150	(Same)
Translated poetry (per line)	to 50	(None)	9- 14	(4- 14)
Works on literature, art, criticism	10	(Same)	150-400	(Same)
Theoretical science literature	None	(10)	150-300	(Same)
Popular science literature	None	(50)	100-300	(Same)
Industrial and technical literature	None	(10)	80-200	(100-200)
Textbooks	None	(25-400)	100-250	(Same)
Translated scientific works	None	(Same)	30-100	(40- 80)

Note: On translations, the rates specified above are increased
by 25% for translations from rare languages and ancient
languages and by 15% for translations from Russian and
other languages of the U.S.S.R. into external foreign
languages.

Table 22

Books and Pamphlets - By Republic Where Published
(All languages; priced and free)

(In each pair of numbers the upper is the number of titles
and lower is the number of copies)

	1950	1957	1961
Total	43,060	58,792	73,999
	820,529,000	1,047,266,000	1,119,400,000
Armenian	830	964	1,088
SSR	4,878,000	6,561,000	6,833,000
Azerbaijan	1,030	1,093	1,326
SSR	7,967,000	9,489,000	10,990,000
Belorussian	616	928	1,638
SSR	12,559,000	16,300,000	18,966,000
Estonian	942	1,119	1,589
SSR	5,372,000	6,595,000	8,014,000
Georgian	1,380	1,932	2,621
SSR	8,181,000	11,171,000	12,447,000
Kazakh	776	1,194	1,516
SSR	11,489,000	12,953,000	16,020,000
Kirghiz	358	813	880
SSR	2,853,000	4,896,000	5,079,000
Latvian	1,314	1,505	2,485
SSR	9,301,000	10,917,000	13,837,000
Lithuanian	1,073	1,828	1,896
SSR	8,144,000	11,581,000	13,807,000
Moldavian	554	781	1,311
SSR	4,457,000	6,307,000	9,374,000
RSFSR	28,486	38,141	45,586
	646,798,000	822,517,000	851,788,000
Tajik	347	509	675
SSR	2,784,000	3,610,000	4,093,000
Turkoman	310	600	634
SSR	2,344,000	3,743,000	3,145,000
Ukrainian	4,136	5,808	8,718
SSR	77,649,000	100,647,000	120,895,000
Uzbek	908	1,577	2,033
SSR	15,753,000	19,979,000	24,663,000

XVI. COPYRIGHT

On every appropriate occasion we presented the problem
of international copyright, and argued the disadvantages of
the Soviet Union's present position as a non-adherent to the
Universal Copyright Convention and the advantages, both
national and international, that would flow from their joining the UCC. We spoke of the Universal Copyright Convention
rather than the Berne Convention because joining the UCC
would require fewer changes from present copyright practice
within the Soviet Union. The resulting discussions usually
were frank and direct, but in most instances the directors
or editors-in-chief of publishing houses would protest at the
outset that this was properly a matter for discussion on the
governmental level and not between publishers or representatives of publishers' organizations.

Nevertheless, our arguments were received politely and
patiently in almost every conference, and usually there was
rebuttal of varying kind, strength and conviction. We were
surprised to find that many of the Soviet publishing officials
were uninformed or even misinformed on general facts and
issues as well as on critical technical points. Obviously
most of them had not been exposed to, nor much interested in,
the true position and posture of the U.S.S.R. on the international copyright scene, except as it involved their "sister
socialist republics." Hence our many discussions served not
only to give fairly wide ventilation to the problem of copyright, but also to inform and often to correct certain widely-
held misconceptions.

Our most useful discussions in this area seemed to be
those with Mrs. Ye. A. Furtseva, Minister of Culture; Mr.
S. K. Romanovsky, Chairman of the State Committee for Cultural
Relations with Foreign Countries; and Mr. A. P. Rybin, Chief
of the Main Administration of Publishing Houses (Glavizdat)
in the Ministry of Culture. At the end of a frank and spirit-

ed but friendly debate with Mrs. Furtseva, which took place
at the very end of our stay in the Soviet Union, she stated
that perhaps her Ministry needed more information on the
legal technicalities, the publishing problems and the economic
issues involved. She then went on to suggest that a special
committee might be appointed to investigate the matter. Following this, we had another session with Mr. Rybin, who had
attended the meeting with Minister Furtseva, at which the
position of each side was examined in some detail.

In the publishing houses, nearly everyone agreed that
the present situation was not a happy one. Nearly everyone
also agreed that the publication of translations without the
consent of the author and without royalty payments was wrong
in principle. Several officials agreed in principle that the
U.S.S.R. should become a member of the UCC, but they were
very wary of the practical difficulties (political, legal and
economic) involved. When the subject had been broached successfully, we usually found ready interest and willingness to
discuss it within a limited frame of authority and responsibility. Only once was the discussion cut off by the Soviet
chairman's saying that it was not a proper subject for discussion at that time, place and level.

So in the end we felt that these discussions had had
much value to both sides - that they had paved the way to a
better understanding of the true issues involved and a better
appreciation of the interests on each side of each issue. We
are encouraged to feel that our discussions might even lead
to a reconsideration of the problem by the appropriate officials and organizations in the U.S.S.R.

For those who have a special interest in this matter,
the balance of this chapter is devoted to a summary of our
arguments and of the Soviet counter-arguments, as we understood them.

Copyright - The Position of the U.S. Delegation

The position of our delegation on the international copyright problem and the publishing issues involved between the U.S.S.R. and the U.S.A. can be summarized as follows:

1. In the absence of a copyright agreement between our nations, no U. S. publisher can now gain an exclusive right to publish an English-language translation of any U.S.S.R. book. Without the protection of an exclusive right, producing translations is risky, because two or more U. S. publishers might decide at the same time to translate a popular Soviet book. This risk factor greatly restricts the number of U.S.S.R. books being published in translation, and as a result contemporary Russian literature and many important scientific and technical works are almost unknown in the English-speaking world. If this situation could be corrected, the number of translations published outside the Soviet Union would quickly increase by several fold.

2. A bilateral copyright treaty between the U.S.S.R. and the U.S.A. would not be an effective solution to the present problem. While this might provide exclusive translation rights to U.S. publishers, it would not bind English-language publishers in Great Britain, Canada, Australia and elsewhere. Hence, world English-language markets would still be harmfully divided, and especially those for scientific books where such markets are usually small to begin with. Since a bilateral agreement would not answer the problem of exclusive English-language translation rights, the adherence of the U.S.S.R. to the UCC seems to be the only real solution.

3. On the economic side, it is wrong to think in terms of past and present experience when considering the question of the future balance or imbalance of royalty payments. It must be admitted that under present conditions the balance of such payments might be against the U.S.S.R. However, under a binding international copyright agreement this situation

would probably change immediately to a monetary balance in favor of the U.S.S.R. for the following reasons:

(a) Royalties would be payable only under contracts for _new_ translations negotiated after the agreement had been signed. No royalty payments could be required on translations published prior to the agreement.

(b) Under an agreement that allowed exclusive rights, the number of U.S.S.R. titles translated and published in English-language editions would be immediately and greatly increased in the U.S.A., Great Britain and elsewhere. This would probably also be the case for other major western languages.

(c) With royalties based on list prices, and with list prices in the U.S.A. and Great Britain three to four times higher than in the U.S.S.R. in terms of the 90 kopeck = one dollar exchange rate, royalties earned by the U.S.S.R. at the same percentage rates would also be three to four times greater on each Soviet title.

(d) Royalties earned by the U.S.S.R. on copyrighted musical works, and particularly from recording and performance rights, would be heavily in favor of the Soviet Union.

4. Since English has become the second language of most of the large and important areas of the world where Russian is little known, the translation of significant Russian books into English is the only way in which such books can come to be widely known and appreciated in these regions. Exports to these markets would represent about 50% of the total sales of English-language editions of Soviet scientific and technical books produced in the United States.

5. Under present conditions translated editions are published in each country without the permission of, and usually even without the knowledge of, the original authors.

Further, the original authors usually receive no payment whatever for the use of their works. In exceptional cases where some payment is made, there is no systematic nor rational pattern for such payment. This situation is unfair, both morally and financially, to the authors of both countries.

6. The U.S.S.R. is the only major publishing nation of the world that is not a member of either the Berne or the Universal Copyright Convention, and this abstention causes an unfortunate state of anarchy in the book publishing world. The Soviet Union's insular position is not understood in the other major publishing countries, and it is a hindrance to the establishment of good cultural and trading relations in the international world of books.

Copyright - The Soviet Position

Counter-arguments from the U.S.S.R. side, as we understood them, and our rebuttals, can be stated briefly as follows:

1. Since we in the U.S.S.R. publish many more books than you do in translations, and since our editions run much larger than yours, the balance of royalty payments would be very unfavorable to us, and this we cannot afford. The situation would be specially unbearable if we had to pay royalties retroactively on past publications as some Americans visiting the Soviet Union such as Adlai Stevenson and Harold Berman have demanded of us.

Rebuttal: With publishing conditions changed under a copyright agreement, the balance of payment would immediately change in your favor for the reasons stated above. No retroactive payments of royalties on translations already in print would be or could be required if you adhere to the UCC.

2. We are prepared to grant through M.K. exclusive rights for translation of any of our Soviet books to any publishing firm in the U.S.A. It is up to your publishing

172

organizations or your government to provide regulations which
will prevent other publishers from infringing an exclusive
right so granted.

Rebuttal: Under the U.S. anti-trust and restraint-of-
trade laws, we American publishers cannot legally act in combination on a matter such as this. Even if enforcement could
be obtained in the U.S.A., publishers in Great Britain and
Canada, or any other country, would still be free to publish
other English-language translations and thus fractionate
world markets for any given title. Further, we have concrete
evidence that M.K. often tries to place English-language translation rights with British and U.S. firms simultaneously and
this practice could not be controlled by any action of the
United States.

3. We should not give a U.S. publisher exclusive
world rights to an English-language translation because this
would mean that a book could be translated and sold in the
U.S. alone and denied to readers in other English-speaking
countries. Each English-speaking country should have the
right to produce its own edition. (Obviously this argument
was in contradiction to the immediately foregoing argument,
and it was not advanced by the same person.)

Rebuttal: No publisher would be foolish enough to
restrict sales to his own country. Even the remote possibil-
ity of such foolish behavior could be prevented by having
each translation contract require that the translated edition
must be made available for sale in all the major English-
speaking countries simultaneously.

4. Payment of royalties on translations would greatly
increase the prices of books for our students and readers.
As a nation dedicated to the production of low-priced books
for everyone, we cannot pay the high royalties on translations which are customary in the capitalist countries.

Rebuttal: There are no "customary" royalty rates
among UCC member countries. Royalties are negotiable on

each separate publication, and the rates would be low for your large-size, sure-sales editions. Further, the rates customarily are based on the price of the translated edition, which would be low in your case. Thus you would usually pay lower rates on a low list price, and this would add little to the prices of your books.

5. We want our books translated free of cost by our "sister socialist republics" and by the poorer, underdeveloped nations of the world which cannot afford to pay royalties to anyone. If we joined the UCC, we would have to abandon this policy and charge the high royalty rates set by the capitalist nations.

Rebuttal: Not so. Adherence to the UCC does not require payments of royalties at any rate or in any case. You would still be able to license translations free of charge to any country and in any language of your choice. As to your relations with your "sister socialist republics," it should be noted that Czechoslovakia is a member of the UCC and Poland, Czechoslovakia, Hungary, Rumania and Bulgaria are members of the Berne Convention. These memberships seem not to have hurt their publishing relationships within the Communist bloc or with outside nations, both developed and underdeveloped.

6. If we were to join the UCC, we should have to make drastic changes in our domestic copyright laws in order to conform to the practices of the capitalist nations. For example, we would not want to change our term of copyright from the life of the author plus fifteen years to life and fifty years as usually allowed in the Western European countries.

Rebuttal: Actually UCC makes few rigid requirements of its member nations. Its underlying principle is that each member nation shall give foreign authors the same protection and treatment as are given its own national authors. There are very few minimum requirements, but the term of copyright is one of them. The UCC requires a minimum term of twenty-five years from date of publication. Thus only in the small number of cases where Soviet authors fail to live ten years after the publication of their work, would there need to be any change in your present legislation and practice on the copyright term.

7. Your own nation, the U.S.A., for many years was not a member of any international copyright agreement. You took what you wanted when you needed it for your national development. How can you now say that we should not do the same?

Rebuttal: Yes, in our formative years we were guilty of pirating the property of European authors and publishers. But when we had developed a literature of our own and had reached maturity as a nation in the international scene, we reformed our ways in this and several similar matters. Since 1891 foreign authors have been able to copyright their works in the United States, and we were the first of the present 46 members of the UCC. Surely, the U.S.S.R. has reached the point in its national development and its international interests where you would profit by taking a similar course. Many of the new and developing countries of the world such as India, Ghana and Nigeria have joined the UCC already and have a better record in this respect than either the U.S.A. or the U.S.S.R.

XVII. EPILOGUE

This report has attempted to cover much ground as briefly as possible. Each one of us brought a different background of individuality and experience to this study. Out of our common experience in the U.S.S.R. we have presented our joint findings. We have endeavored to stick to essentials and the broad picture, getting into details only when necessary to point up some phase of publishing which seemed to us unusual or of special significance.

Book publishers of the U.S.S.R. and the U.S.A. are alike in that they deal with books and sometimes with magazines, but there are differences which are basic. While we wholeheartedly acknowledge the widespread publishing structure that the U.S.S.R. has developed in a generation or two and the hard working men and women who operate it, no American publisher could be at home in the Soviet system of publishing, with its confinements, controls and lack of direct and rapid response to the demands of the readers of books. The life and spirit of publishing, as we feel it, is lacking in the U.S.S.R. Despite the many parallels and similarities, each publishing scene, editorially, is a world apart.

We close this report with an expression of renewed thanks for the many courtesies shown us during our month's visit in the U.S.S.R.

Academies of Sciences of the Republics, publishing houses, 8, 70, 123-125

Academy of Pedagogical Sciences, 23, 142, 149

Advertising and promotion, inadequacy by U.S. standards, 11, 78-79, 85-86, 90

All-Union Book Chamber, 9, 70, 86, 91-92, 100

American authors, translations, 19, 33, 81-82, 120, 155, 159

American Book Publishers Council, 1, 65

"American Books in Soviet Publishing," by Melville J. Ruggles, 155

American Textbook Publishers Institute, 1, 65

A.P.N. publishing house, 32

Association of American Publishers, 5

Association of Scientific and Technical Publishing Houses (Ontiz), 70, 125, 153

Audiovisual aids, 23, 132

Backlist titles, lack, 11, 83, 89

Belles-lettres publishing, 19-20, 82, 118-122. See also American authors

Berne Convention, on copyright, 35, 37, 168, 172, 174

Bibliographic information, availability, 92, 152

Book information, need for exchange between U.S. and U.S.S.R., 20, 25

Bookmobiles, 85

Books, distinct from pamphlets, 14, 16

Bookstores, 2, 12, 80, 82-85

British publishers, 3, 10, 22, 66

Byelorussian S.S.R.: publishing, 8; Academy of Sciences, 22; establishment of university press, 26; Soviet Encyclopedia, 31

Censorship, unsatisfactory discussions, 10-11, 20, 78

Children's Book House (research), 24

Children's books, 24-25, 70-71, 141-143

Children's Publishing House (Detgiz), 70, 131, 141-142

"Children's World" publishing house, 71, 141, 142

Competitions, for textbook manuscripts, 133, 136, 138

Contract: author's, 34, 77; publishing, 45-50

Control, of publishing, 1, 8, 9, 69, 75. See also Censorship

Copyright law: international, 2, 4, 32; Russian, 42-44, 163-164; U.S. and Russian positions, 35-38, 168-175; on translations, 154-155, 169-174

Curriculum, school, 23, 129-131; in Ukraine, 135-136

Customer access to books, inadequacy, 2, 12, 83-84, 85, 90

Delegation to Russia: members, 1, 3, 64, 65; highlights of changes, 1-2; objectives, 3-4, 65; itinerary and arrangements, 4, 66-67

Delegation visits: to printing plants, 18, 108, 112-117; to belles-lettres publishing houses, 19, 118-121; to science book publishers, 22, 124; to children's book publishers, 24, 141; to university presses, 26; to translation houses, 32-33; to textbook publishers, 128, 131-139

Detgiz, see Children's Publishing House

Detskaya Literatura Publishing House, 24

Dictionary publishing, 27, 150

Discipline, of workers, 111

Distribution: of books, 8-9, 12-13, 78-79, 80-90; of newspapers and magazines, 80, 82, 100; of textbooks, 132-133, 136; of children's books, 142; foreign trade, see Mezhdunarodnaia Kniga. See also Knigotorg

Dom Kniga (House of Books), 12

Editing, in Russia, 74, 77, 133-134, 144-145

Editorial boards and councils, 74, 77, 118-119, 123, 124, 136, 147

Employee benefits, 18, 111; incentives and bonuses, 10, 75, 76, 109

Encyclopedia Dictionary, 27

Encyclopedia publishing, 27-31, 71, 142, 147-150

English, teaching in Russian schools, 66, 130-131, 135, 137, 139

Fiction, see Belles-lettres

Fizmatgiz, see State Publishing House of Literature for Physics and Mathematics

Foreign trade in publications, 17, 36, 100-107.
See also Knigotorg; Mezhdunarodnaia Kniga

Glavizdat (publishing house branch), 69, 71, 72

Glavlit (central censorship agency), 78

Goslitizdat (belles-lettres publishing house),
118, 142

Great Soviet Encyclopedia, 27-28, 147

Hermitage Museum Publishing House, 121

"Higher Schools" publishing house, 144, 145

Income tax withholdings, 110

International Book Year, 3, 5

International Publishers Association, 3, 5

Inventory controls, 11

Journals: scientific and technical, 21, 22, 26,
152; literary, 33; for teachers, 134

Kazakhstan, publishing in, 72, 137-139

Khudozhestvennaya Literatura publishing house, 19

Knigotorg, distribution system, 9, 12, 69, 72, 80-
83, 86-89, 100, 132, 142, 153

Libraries, 90, 126, 152

Literary criticism, 21. See also Belles-lettres

Mail order purchases, 13, 84-85

Manufacture of books, see Printing equipment;
Production

Manuscript acceptance, 47-49

Medgiz, see State Medical Publishing House

Mezhdunarodnaia Kniga (M.K. or Mezh-Kniga),
foreign distribution system, 11, 17, 36, 81,
100-102, 153

Ministry of Culture, U.S.S.R., 69-70

Mir publishing house, 22, 32-33

Mister Twister, 142-143

Moscow: as main publishing center, 69, 118, 119-
120, 131-134; state university press, 26;
printing plant visited, 112-113

Nauka, see U.S.S.R. Academy of Sciences

"New Books Abroad" (journal), 32-33, 126, 152

Novosti, 32

Novye Knigi (New Books) catalog, 100

Ontiz, see Association of Scientific and Technical
Publishing Houses

Ordering system, 86, 89; reorders, 87, 88

Output, number of titles and copies, 1-2, 7, 8,
15, 16, 56-59, 93-95, 98. See also various
types of books

Paper, scarcity, 9, 28, 69, 72, 75, 87, 93

Paperbacks, 97

Pechat' SSSR, 2, 14, 77, 92, 127

Poetry, see Belles-lettres

Postal rates for books, 13

Press Committee: of U.S.S.R. Council of Ministers,
4, 6, 8, 9, 12, 27, 34; Republic level, 6-7, 12

Prices, of books, 2, 15, 36, 53-54, 76, 91, 95-97,
99, 118, 138, 141. See also Delegation visits
to various types of plants

Printing equipment: improved quality, 2, 18;
foreign trade in, 17, 55, 101, 107; allocation,
72, 75, 87. See also Delegation visits to
various types of plants

Production: comparison with U.S., 14-16, 36, 91-
95, 98; organization, 74, 77, 108-117, 145; by
Republic, 167

Profits of publishing houses, use, 10, 23, 75, 80,
109

Progress publishing house, 19, 24, 32, 33

Prosveschcheniye publishing house, 23

Publishers, Russian, proposed visit to U.S., 5,
37, 38

Publishing, organization, 1, 6-9, 68-73

Publishing House for Far Eastern Literature, 21

Publishing House of Foreign Languages, 22, 32, 33,
81, 146, 151, 152-153

Publishing House of Foreign Literature, 22, 32, 33,
126, 146, 151-152, 158

Publishing House of Oriental Literature, 70

Publishing House of the Ministry of Higher and
Specialized Education, 153

Publishing houses: administrative structure, 1, 6, 10-11, 74-79; three categories, 7-8, 68-71, 73; relation to printing plants, 108

Publishing in the U.S.S.R., by Boris I. Gorokhoff, 68, 78, 127

Publishing industry, handbook, 51-52

Quality of manufacture, 18, 24, 97

Regional economic council, 108; of Leningrad, 111-112

Reprints and reissues, 14, 16, 87

Research centers, for children's books, 24-25

Retail sales, 83-84, 92; volume, 80, 81

Retirement, age and benefits, 110-111

Roman-Gazeta (Moscow magazine), 119

Royalties, 34, 76, 77, 161-166; on textbooks, 23, 138-139; for belles-lettres, 39-41; on translations, 154-155; under international copyright, 37, 170-174

Salaries, in publishing, 76, 96-97, 109-111, 133-134, 138, 154

Science fiction, 22, 32

Scientific and technical books, 21-22, 123-127; translations, 155-156, 160

Selection of titles, 21, 77, 123, 124, 125, 126

Small Soviet Encyclopedia, 27

Soiuzpechat', magazine and newspaper distribution system, 80, 82, 100

Soyuzkniga, distribution system, 9, 11, 12. See also Knigotorg

Spirit of publishing, different in U.S.S.R., 176

Sputnik magazine, 32

State Medical Publishing House (Medgiz), 71

State Publishing House of Dictionaries, 150

State Publishing House of Literature for Physics and Mathematics (Fizmatgiz), 21, 125-126, 146, 153

State Scientific Encyclopedia Publishing House of the U.S.S.R., 27, 71, 147

State Textbook Publishing House (Uchpedgiz), 128-136

Statistical definitions, in U.S.S.R., 92-93. See also UNESCO statistical standards

Surplus books, 13, 86-87

Teacher training, 131-132, 138

Textbooks: scientific and medical, 21, 71;
    elementary and secondary school, 23, 71,
    128-140; higher education, 26, 71, 144-146;
    translations, 153

Thematic plans, 10, 74-77, 84, 86, 118, 123

Translations, 22, 32-33, 119-120, 126, 151-
    160; of children's books, 24, 142; of
    Soviet books, 36; of textbooks, 138, 144,
    145, 146; protection by copyright, 154-155,
    169-174. See also American authors, translations

Uchpedgiz, see State Textbook Publishing House

Ukraine, organization of publishing, 71-72,
    134-136

UNESCO statistical standards, 2, 14, 95

Union of Soviet Writers, 11, 19, 35, 70, 82,
    120-121

Universal Copyright Convention, 35, 37, 66,
    168-170, 172-175

University presses, 26, 146, 153

U.S.-U.S.S.R. Exchanges Agreement, 3, 63, 65

U.S.S.R. Academy of Sciences, publishing house
    (Nauka), 8, 21, 22, 70, 82, 123, 153

U.S.S.R. Committee for Coordination of Scientific
    Research, publishing houses, 125, 146

Warehousing and shipping, 12-13, 87-89

Workbooks, 132, 134

Workers' unions, 10, 74, 76, 111

Youth Guard Publishing House, 142